The brightness of Darkness of an African

Knowing the Past, Living the Present, and
Hoping for the Future

James Yamkela Qeqe
The New Voice of Africa

PUBLICATION
CONSULTANTS
We Believe In The Power Of Authors

PO Box 221974 Anchorage, Alaska 99522-1974
books@publicationconsultants.com, www.publicationconsultants.com

ISBN Number: 978-1-59433-851-9
eBook ISBN Number: 978-1-59433-852-6

Library of Congress Catalog Card Number: 2019933034

Manufactured in the United States of America

Dedication

Dedicated to a friend of mine EMMANUEL SIM 'NATHI' MABELANE, to my late classmates YAMKELA LEVE and QHAMANI NGANASE and to all those who seek the truth of our past, the suffered and suffering Africans and African Americans. To PUSELETSO SAULI, the FW de KLERK FOUNDATION, STEVE BIKO FOUNDATION, the THABO MBEKI FOUNDTION and the NELSON MANDELA FOUNDATION. To a great friend of Steve Bantu Biko Professor. Rev. BARNEY PITYANA, Archbishop Emeritus DESMOND TUTU who both continues to serve and pray for Africa in silence. TO JOHN KANI THE LEGEND. To the MARTIN LUTHER KING JR FOUNDATION. To my secretary MZIKAZI JAZA, and ARNOLD ASAVELA KHALIPA my organizer. **African Love Your Self!**

From the Author's Desk.

This at some point is a personal account, may and may not be regarded as typical. I have done a number of researches regarding racism, xenophobia, sexism and even tribalism. Mostly in South Africa. I have concentrated on those people, who in a way would like to remain anonymous for personal reasons, who have suffered in one way or the other, but we know a number of people, who still even today, remain silent because they are still ashamed of the past. I hope that in looking carefully at those who have fought a good fight in our struggles, both in South Africa and in the United States of America, we may appreciate the effort and strength with which they courageously stood firm for truth and their beliefs.

Our intentions, (I and the editor) are to help to bring about peace in the world, by retelling the story. It is indeed by retelling the story that we would be able to help the world heal from all these wounds, of hatred and of violence.

Undoubtedly and unceasingly, we put in to mind that, there are experts who can tell the story better than we can, but nevertheless, we contribute to those who can. The story may be told, but if they are no intentions behind the story, still the story remains dead and meaningless. Through the book, we have referred to those who have both suffered from the struggles, both known and unknown. This may give offence to some individuals, but still, truth has to be told in the end. Most of all, we want not our history to die in our hands, we must tell the history to generations to come. If it dies in our hands, if the generations to come know nothing about our history, pleasant or painful, we would be blamed for it. In fact we should be blamed.

Finally, this research was not done by experts, at the same time; the author is the king in this genre. Some experts might argue with some of the definitions or the weight to different 'treatments'. But this is my particular view. It's my book.

And It's Emmanuel's too. I'd like to thank him for giving me the insight to write it. Ke a leboga 'NATHI'.

Contents

CHAPTER ONE

The deposition of our brethren

It was always my desire to have more connection with African people, more especially those who have been deposited in other countries during the different struggles in the world. Many things and events had led to the deposition of African people to other foreign lands, treating them as inferior. Well this has originated from of old. "You're black, you're nothing." After I have worked with George Eden Bess in the Southern African Region, that was after the Second World War, I and my wife Tsholofelo had a very interesting conversation about our African brethren who are in other countries. Well the intention was to investigate if they really know their history and origin. My father always told me this one thing in life, "Son, whatever you do in life, do not forget who you are and who you want to be." He would say.

I felt it was my duty rather than my assignment to make sure that every African, know who they arc, where're they from and where're they going to. Because in life two things are important, to know where you're from and where you're going to. As GEB and I were married to our wives for about thirty six years now, I felt like it was my responsibility to invite him to this research of 'African Americans'. So he agreed and invited me over to Germany.

"You're a great man Chungu, I hope you'll get what you're looking for." Tsholofelo said.

"I will try my best my love." I responded.

So I went to Germany, to meet my best historian friend, George Eden Bess known as GEB in Africa. He fetched me from the airport. But before that I waited for GEB, at the airport for about an hour or so. After waiting for that long, a man touched my shoulder from behind.

"Hello Chungu! How do you do?"

"Eden, you're late, as usual!" I said.

"Is that your way to greet an old friend? Come give me a hug!" he said with that smile which I first saw in South Africa. It was not at all different, after twenty-five years that was the smile I recognized. "After all, it was you who was always late, not me. Maybe I'm just returning the favor." My passion was always to change the world. But my mother was always at my side, telling me that I cannot change the world unless I change my country Zambia. I could not understand the words then, until few years later. All she meant was that, as 'charity begins at home', you can not at all start saving another person's life unless you show that impression at home. It was lovely to see Juliet again after long time ever since we last saw each other in Africa.

"You still look beautiful Mrs. GEB." I said.

"Hello to you too Chungu. "She replied.

It was also my first time to meet the offspring of my beloved friend. George Junior and the little Tsholofelo. My wife would love to see her, she was so cute.

Life is 50/50, life gives, life takes. It all depends on how it starts to you. You should only be patient. So we went to the States and we were welcomed by the lady who had been a history lecturer for many years. It was segregation which we first found out about in the States. We were so interested in doing the research. We then visited Sir Philip James who was one of those who were totally against segregation and other immoral acts against humanity. Well South Africa also suffered under these immoralities of racism, segregation and even xenophobia. All these can be classified as 'lacking in knowledge and understanding'.

Now we were welcomed by Josephina James at her father's house. We were in Alabama.

"Please take a sit, my father will be with you in a minute, can I offer you something to drink meanwhile?" Said Josephina.

"We shall be waiting, water will be fine thanks." Replied George.

Mr. James' house looked like a library; especially his family room, he was one of the Professors in the local University. His house was very decent, it had a dignity. It was quiet, as ever. It looked like a Pope's office, although I've never seen it. It had a nice picture of the great man Martin Luther King Jr and other civil rights leaders of the municipal bus boycott in Montgomery, Alabama, riding an integrated bus, December 1956. There was also a picture of Mr. President Thabo Mvuyelwa Mbeki of South Africa, and another of Reverend Dr Martin Luther King Jr waving to the crowds gathered in Washington on 28 August 1963.

There was also his famous speech framed and nailed on the wall, with bold attracting words 'I HAVE A DREAM'. Immediately after reading those words, I could hear his voice addressing the crowds gathered together, cheering at him and throwing their hats up as in graduation. After all I had a vision of him waving unceasingly, smiling to the crowds. Also a picture of President Nelson Rholihlahla 'Dalibhunga' Mandela was there, on his day of release from Victor Verster prison in 1990 accompanied by his wife Mama Winnie Madikizela Mandela.

Above all there was also a painted picture of Pope John the XXIII with the inscription 'Open the doors of the church, so that the Holy Spirit may enter.'

"Your glass of water gentlemen. Said Josephina."

"Thank you." We both said.

At last the man appeared, Sir James. As he was coming in, he appeared with his long black and white beard which moved back and forth as he was entering the room. He was wearing a white satin caftan like an angel, and fur-trimmed black hat. As he passed each shelf of books he was looking at us, coming towards us. He was tall, but not that tall. He walked slowly, his hands clasped behind his back. And as he came closer to us, I could see that part of his face not hidden by the beard looked cut from stone. The nose was sharp and pointed, the cheekbones ridged. His lips were as red as a coal, the eyebrows were thick and eyes dark as if painted. He took off his hat and put it down, and smiled with his hand stretched to greet us.

"Good morning gentlemen."Sir James said.

"Sir James."

"How do you do sir?" I asked with a smile.

"That is Pope John the XXIII." Sir James said pointing at the painting."

"I see." Said George.

"He is the one who called the council of Vatican II, to revive the church. All the bishops met in the Vatican to discuss the matters of the church. He wanted the priests together with their local bishops to bring the church to the people, if people can't come to church."

"Wow, that's profound Sir James." I said.

Sadly he couldn't live longer to see its fulfillment. His successor Pope Paul VI had to make sure that everything goes as John XXIII had wished. That is why the College of Cardinals had to appoint someone who would not oppose what John XXIII had in mind. So Paul VI had completed the council and he lived longer to see its fulfillment. By the way, are you catholic?"

"Yes, Sir James." We both said.

"Then you should know these things. If you're real catholic. Please take a sit. Anyway you did not come here for church history. Tell me now, why do you want to do this research?"

"Well, Sir James, the church always play a role in the world, it is always involve in every war that I can think of. First, this is Chungu from Zambia, we've been friends and partners since our first research together in Southern Africa. I am George, the one who wrote you a letter."

"I'm pleased to meet you Chungu and George Eden."

"Likewise Sir James."

"Well, I have been motivated by Chungu, that we do this research about the African American brothers. The reason behind this is that, we want to bring truth and knowledge in the world. We want to know about their history and the treatment they received where they have been deposited whether as slaves or something else."

"In the past, many years ago, Africans have been taken by the European countries and the Western countries as well. They took them as slaves, mostly. The earliest-known account of slaves being exported from south-eastern Africa is that of a British trader who called at Port Natal. (Present -day Durban). This was discovered around the 1719, if I am not mistaken."

"How did it go Sir James, what really happened?" I asked.

"Well none of us where there, so we really don't know what happened. But anthropologists and historians such as John Reader, argue that, there they were trading for slaves, with large brass rings, or rather collars, and several other commodities. John Reader also makes note that, around 1783 local chiefs sold enemies captured in war as slaves. And that really contributed to the growth of slaves during that time."

"So, they also played a role in promoting slavery?" Asked George.

"That's correct, Eden".

"Now, in a fortnight they purchased seventy four boys and girls. The early historians and anthropologists are believed to have had a conversation with the slave lords, and they asked them why did they take more staves from Africa than other lands and Islands. The response was "These are better slaves for working than those of Madagascar, being not only blacker but stronger as well. Because also they made their work much easier and they would only send them to the fields to harvest there for their own good."Such was their life!

CHAPTER TWO

Segregation in USA

"So Sir James, how was segregation in the States?" I asked.

"Segregation in the United States of America was depressing. In the 1960s was an extraordinary time or period if you like, of social unrest and protest action and activities by ordinary people. Mainly these events occurred in America and Europe, but later on countries like Czechoslovakia, Mexico, New Zealand, Eastern European countries and even Australia were engaged in protest and dissent."

"What does that mean?" George asked.

"They refused to accept the ideas of thinking; expressing difference of opinion." Answered Sir James.

"Oh! I see." George understood.

"There was also what is known as 'Sit-ins'. Have you heard of that before?" Asked Sir James." said George.

"Yes, I have heard of it." I responded.

"Please tell us what you know about it Chungu." Sir James said.

"Those were sits reserved for white people only in public places, such as in restaurants and in buses and many public places you can think of."

"Even in toilets Chungu?" Mr. James asked with a sarcastic smile.

"Yes, Mr. James, even in toilets." We all laughed after that.

"You are quite correct Mr. Chungu, sit-ins were very common form of protests during the civil rights movement. Activists would protest against segregationist laws by deliberately sitting in places reserved for whites. In Greensboro the first sit-in started the sit-in movement. That was in the 1960s still."

"That's sad." I said.

"Well it doesn't end there. Madam Rosa Parks was one of the bravest women ever. She also played a role in the Bus boycott in Montgomery, Alabama. History records that it was on Thursday December 1, 1955 when Rosa Parks boarded a city bus, moved to the black where African Americans were required to sit. But all sits were taken so she sat in one toward the middle of the bus."

"Was that sit for whites." I asked.

"Because it was towards the middle of the bus, not really was it for whites. But because the seats were all occupied, that means from front seats till the middle. I suppose the black seats were also occupied, for the fact that she sat towards the middle. When a white man boarded the bus, the driver ordered Rosa to vacate her seat for him."

"Was the driver a white man?" I asked.

"Obviously!" said Sir James.

"What would you do if you were in Rosa's shoes Sir James?" Asked George.

"Honestly, I would have done the same, in fact I would have made things worse by giving the driver a smack."

Haha! We all laughed.

"There was nothing unusual in his request..."

"Was it a request or a command?" I asked.

"A command rather, but on that day fateful, Rosa Parks refused to move. What a havoc she had caused! She had not planned to resist on that day but, as she later said, she had 'decide that I would have to know once and for all what rights I had as a human being and citizen.'..."

"Wow, she was really brave." George said.

"When her moment came she seized it and with this act of resistance launched the Montgomery bus boycott movement and inspired the modern civil rights struggle for freedom and equality. And those were the inequalities between black and white Americans."

"Now was this happening only in America?" I asked.

"What?"

"The inequalities and stuff?"

"Not only in America, also in South Africa. They experienced the very same thing at the very same time. In South Africa it all began around the 1940s. People really suffered."

"Tell us your experienced on segregation Sir 'Jay', what other things had happened during those days?" George asked.

"I remember one occasion, we went to the city, and it was my two African friends and myself. When we got into the city, the two police officers who were standing against the wall of the one building, called them. We went to them respectfully, and they had asked me to leave "leave the 'Negros behind...'" "They are my friends, I cannot leave them not with you more especially."

"You were very defensive Sir 'Jay."I said.

"Defensive, I don't know, but protective, Yes! They were my friends. The police officer then asked me "What kind of a white man associate with black men? Are you insane?" So I said in reply, "If they are not human, then kill me in their place, but if they are human beings, then why do you persecute us".

"Wow, Sir James."George said.

"So the police officers ordered me to be arrested with them."

"Where you arrested?" George asked.

"That's what I'm saying."Responded Sir James. I remember the words of the great Mahatma Gandhi, "Be the change you would like to see in the world."

"Tell us more Sir James!" I said.

"Young people – particularly students, formed a major part of all protests movements, both in organizing and taking part in them. The youth had played a very significant role in these protests. Even in Vietnam, the youth called for the withdrawal of the American troops from the war, to come back and explain why they did what they did."

"I am also interested in that. Would you say more on that Sir James?" I asked.

"Not now Chungu. Let me first finish this. Besides, there's a good friend of mine who can tell the story better than me, Luke. He's aging now, but still kicking alive."

"I am still listening Mr. James."Said George.

"George Eden Bess was listening very attentively, he reminds me when we were still in Africa, listening to those old men who loved their land like no body's business. Mpumezi, Abner, Alberto and even the great Kamala. I miss them a lot, but I wonder if they are still in this land of the living."

"Around the 1960s the "baby boom" generation meaning those born after the Second World War, were going to universities in large numbers. Most of them were mainly white and some from the middle class. Yet still in the 1960s they came to question the way things were. A minority were to develop a counter-culture known as the hippies who advocated the use of drugs, free love and living in communities. Many ideas which seemed so radical at the time: the sexual revolution, abortion, gender equality, were to quietly become part of the mainstream Western world in the 1970s."

"What about violence Sir James?" I asked.

"Good question Chungu. That was something else as well. Radicalism was one of the most noticeable features of protest in the 1960s."

"What do you mean by that Mr. James?" I asked.

"By that I mean a form of being extreme, desiring extreme reform and changes."

"Now I see." I added.

"In the beginning all followed the non-violent direct action or civil disobedience model of Martin Luther King Jnr, and the early civil rights movement in the American South. However, there were also black riots in large American cities, caused by the frustration of urban black residents, whose lives had not been improved with the passing outside of civil rights legislation. Above all, in August 1968 the anti- Vietnam War protests outside the Democratic Party Convention in Chicago became chaotic, with scenes of violence between police and demonstrators."

"That's very tragic Sir James."

"It was." He said.

"I think we should get going now." George said.

"So we will go to Luke tomorrow morning?"

"Thumbs up Mr. James! I said.

"Oh Yes! Sir James, we will see you early in the morning."

"But wait let me book an appointment with him first, he's a very busy man you know!"

Mr. James then headed to the green telephone which was not very far from him, on the desk in the corner. "Yes… may I please speak to Luke Theron?"

"He's not in yet, may I asked who's this?" The voice said in the telephone.

"I am his old friend and colleague, Philip James."

"Oh Yes! I know where he is, do you have a pencil and something to right on?" the voice asked.

"Just a minute…."

"Got a pencil? It's No. 55 Kensington Colchester. Got that? Double five!"

"Many thanks, I shall pay him a visit. Is he working there this week?"

"Yes, until next week."

"Awesome, good bye. Gentlemen, we shall see each other tomorrow. Drive safely."

"Good bye Sir, James."

CHAPTER THREE

Rejection of non-violence protest

We then left Sir James and his daughter behind. With hope that we shall see him on the following day. I was looking forward to meeting Mr. Luke Theron.

"Do you still remember Mr. Mpumezi, Chungu?" asked George.

"How can I forget him? I still remember all of them. Mr. Abner, Alberto, Ma Makutso and even the great man himself Kamala. I miss them."

"Those were the days my friend, those were the days!"

We then went to Sir James on the following day, so that he takes us to Luke Theron his old friend. It was a very rainy morning.

"Are you ready gentlemen?" he asked.

"Ready when you are Sir!" I said.

Sir James then drove us to Kensington Colchester to see Mr. Theron.

"Appointment with Mr. Theron?" asked the secretary.

"Yes, I am Philip James. Is he in?" said Sir James.

"Yes. He's expecting you, sir. Shall I take your raincoats?"

The secretary then gave the Raincoats to the powerful-looking doorman and put the rain coats on coat-hangers and hung them up on three of the rows of hooks beside the door.

"Would you follow me gentlemen?" she asked.

We then followed her, it was a very narrow corridor of freshly painted clapboard with a tall, double window. The floor had an ugly old red carpet that turned to look like an old gravel road. The passage ended in two facing doors marked '1' and '2'. The secretary knocked at room 1 and stood aside for us to enter. I must say, it was a pleasant very light room, close-carpeted in dove-grey Wilton. A small bright fire burned under an Adam mantelpiece, which bore a number of silver and gold trophies and five photographs in leather frames. One of Malcolm X, the second was of Stokely Carmichael, the next of the Black Panther Party embalm, and the other two were very unusual, one of a nice-looking woman and the other of three nice-looking children. There was a central table with a bowl of flower and four comfortable club chairs on either side of the fire. No desk or filing cabinets, nothing official looking.

"Good morning gentlemen." Luke said.

"I heard that you're keeping busy this side." Said Phillip.

"James, I am trying my best, I have been trying to be busy ever since I passed school." We all laughed after he said that.

"Please, allow me to introduce my friends. This is George Eden Bess, he's from Germany, and this is Chungu Mumba a Zambian."

"I am pleased to meet you gentlemen." Said Luke.

"Likewise Mr. Theron." We both said.

"Tell me now, what are you here for?" he asked.

"These guys are doing their research on the struggles in the US. They want to know everything."

"Well, I don't know about that. We try to forget these things because of the painful past. We blacks were always treated very badly in all over the world. Not only us though, the Red Indians who are believed to have occupied the American land before all else, also the Jews who were most persecuted by Hitler, Heinrich Himmler the Waffen-SS, Ernst Rohm of Sturmabteilung and Joseph Goebbels right hand man of Adolf Hitler and Nazi propaganda Minister, who once described the Jews in pre-Holocaust Germany November 2, 1939 as 'These are no longer humans, these are animals.'"

"What made them less humans?" I asked.

"Good question Chungu, meaning they were humans at first." George added.

"Probably he would say their Jewness." James said.

"It's just like Adolf, who claimed that 'black people are nothing but freak of nature. 'Maybe it was because of the color of the skin, because it was in a white man's mind that if you're black you're inferior. I was very grateful to my white friends, including Phillip, for being friends to us and for being there in the times of need. We had many white friends and some of them were deceitful more than friendly."

"Why do you say that Mr. Theron? I asked.

"Some pretended to be friends whereas they knew that they were not." He said.

"I still don't get it." George added.

"Some police officers had asked our so called 'white friends' to be our friends, so that they can easily catch every movement we made. Probably they were paid. "

"I was one of those who had been asked." Sir James said.

"You also!" Said George.

"But good friends like Phillip James, came to let us know that we're under watch. It was very difficult in those days. Some of our friends 'white friends' were very close to us just to know everything about us, even family matters. Only to find out later on that they were trapping us to sink into the mud."

"Shame on them." I said.

"Among many thousands of people Anne Moody was an activist. She took part in many civil rights activists like the famous Woolworth luncheon sit-in."

"She was white?" George asked.

"Yes. She was white; I am trying to prove to you that not all white people hated us. Or rather not all of them looked us down, some of them they believed in us and were praying for us time and again. Most of them were afraid to show that they were against of all the bad things done to us blacks."

"What were they afraid of." I asked.

"Rejection!" Mr. Theron said.

"I don't comprehend." Said George.

"They were afraid that their own mates would treat them like us. They were scared that they might be rejected in the community by other white people. So it was only the bravest who would take that initiative to be rejected by the community for blacks!"

"I now understand." George said.

"So, Anne participated in the March on Washington District Columbia on 28 August 1963. Just shortly after we sang a couple of songs it was announced that the march to the Lincoln Memorial was about to start. Other thousands of people just took off, leaving most of their leaders on the podium. It was kind of funny in a way to watch the leaders run to overtake the march. The way some of them had been leading the people in the past, perhaps the people were better off leading themselves, I thought!"

"By the time...."

Sir Theron was interrupted by a telephone call."

"Hello, Luke Theron speaking. Yes. Awesome, thank you very much, highly appreciated. Good bye now.... What was I saying again?

"By the time..." I said.

"By the time what?" Luke asked.

"That's what you last said. We don't know 'by the time what."

"I can't remember. Any way, we got to Lincoln Memorial; there were already thousands of people there. I sat on the grass and listened to the speakers, to discover we had heroes who had been dreaming to change the lives of others. Not just leaders who lead people because they see like. Moreover I also discovered that, we would change the world if we would be united."

"Many people had contributed to the struggle, I believe so. Tell us more about the roles that were played by other leaders." I said.

"Even artists had contributed to the struggle. Mahalia Jackson a gospel singer, she also sang just before King's speech during the 1963 March on Washington. Sources say she persuaded King Jr to drop his prepared speech and speak about his dream."

"Wait a minute. Are you saying the speech 'I have a dream' was not prepared?" I asked.

"That's what they say." Luke said.

"That's incredible. I am impressed." Said Geroge.

"It is true that when you speak from the heart, people not only hear what you say, but comprehend it. Because if you speak not from the heart, people only hear what you say, but it has no place in their hearts because it has no place in yours first."

"Wow, I like the sound of that." I said.

"Malcolm X also played a role in the struggle. As you said many people had played a role in the struggle."

"Tell us about him." George said.

George Eden Bess had not changed much, every time he hears something interesting he can't wait until he hears more about it. I did not know if that was something good to do or what.

"Malcolm X was a member of the Nation Islam- and was influenced by the teachings of Elijah Mohammad."

"Elijah Mohammad?" I said.

"Yes, Elijah Mohammad was a black religious leader who led the Nation of Islam (NOI) from 1934 until his death in 1975. He was a mentor to Malcolm X, Louis Farrakhan and Mohammad Ali, as well as his own son, Warith Deen Mohammad."

"Is that so?" I asked.

"Yes, so Malcolm X's father was also anti-racist. He was then murdered by members of a white racist group. He was placed in foster homes. Malcolm did well in school, so they say, and was very wise."

"Now I am interested in the 'X', where does it come from or what does it stand for?" George asked.

"Well, as far as I know it did not stand for anything, but it was symbolic. Malcolm X was formerly Malcolm Little. The 'X' was symbolic of the identity stolen from African slaves."

"Is that so?" George said

"Yes George. So now he and Martin were very non-violent people. Martin Luther King wrote 'Non-violent resistance… avoids not only external physical violence but also internal violence of spirit. The non-violent resister not only refuses to shoot his opponent, but he also refuses to hate him."

"Is that so"? I asked.

"Yes, Chungu, it's powerful isn't?"

"It is more that Sir Luke." I said.

"It was written somewhere, 'As a theologian, Martin Luther King reflected often on his understanding of non-violence…True pacifism,' or nonviolent resistance. King wrote, 'is a courageous confrontation of evil by the power of love."

"How do you describe racism Sir Luke?" George asked.

Mr. James was so quite as if he was not at all in the room. Until we realized that he was sleeping.

"Mr. James!" I called.

"Leave him." Mr. Theron said.

"Before I answer your question. The belief was in the heart of the nonviolent civil rights movement that protests and suffering would force society to deal with its evil structure. Around 1958, Martin had won a major battle in

Montgomery and was building national support. He focused on promoting his philosophy of nonviolence. Above all his strategy won him many followers, but many questioned his policy of convincing blacks to love their white enemies. Well that could have been because of he was the man of God, Christ teaches us to love and pray for our enemies."

"Was not that unfair Mr. Theron?" George asked.

"Opponents claimed this placed an unfair and intolerable psychological burden on the victims of oppression. That is why Malcolm X said 'Nonviolence but self-defense.'"

"So in other words, he meant that if someone beats you up, you should beat bounce?" I asked.

"But it was more in police officers. He should start, not the other way round. Malcolm focused his criticism on the failure of white people to treat black people as human beings. That and that alone was the heart of his critique. Nothing sophisticated or special about it, just a mere talk- telling the truth as it is. This was the crime that whites did not want to hear about, and few blacks had the courage to confront. James H. Cone also takes note that white people enslaved blacks for about 244 years, segregated them for another 100 years. Lynched them all along the way whenever and wherever whites had a mind to demonstrate their absolute power over blacks..."

"...and the question was 'How could American whites exclude blacks and other people of color from political process and yet say that this nation is the land of the free? How could white Christians treat blacks Christians as brutes and still claim love as their central religious principle? How could white police officers brutally damaged the hearts of blacks and claimed that they were protecting the nation with fairness and equality? How? How? How!!!'" Mr. Sir James said, as we thought he was sleeping.

After he had said those touching words, there was silence in the room, and that silence was not just a normal silence, it was tense and I bet, that was the silence experienced by those who stood by the cross of the Lord when he said... "Father, into your hands I commend my spirit."

"Gentlemen let us go, before the sun sets." Mr. James said.

"Should we come tomorrow again?" George asked.

"You can come tomorrow again, if you like. I'll take you to one of our local priests who will tell you his side of the story. Remember the church is always involved in these conflicts and wars. The church has existed long ago, not to be there for people to go to when they have nothing better to do, but to help them find the true meaning of their purpose in life. And that is our calling in life, to know, love and serve God our creator."

"Which priests are going to?" Mr. James asked.

"Father Bryan M."

"I see."

"Have a blessed day gentlemen."

African Americans were encouraged to be proud of their African Heritage, because it has been lost in their lives. What could have resulted to that? Was it pride? Or was it because they have forgotten who they are? Or maybe they did not know in the first place. But no! None of the above, it was because of oppression of the whites to blacks, it was oppression of white to other people of color. Oppression! Oppression! Oppression! But truly how can we continue saying we are equal whereas all these things keep on happening in our watch?

CHAPTER FOUR

The Black Panther Party

On the following day, we went to see the priest, Fr. Bryan M who also experienced these tragic sufferings. Fr. Bryan had been a priest for 30 years, and had been serving in the mother church till present day. He was not that old, but you could see that he had lived many days.

"Brothers in Christ, welcome." Fr. Bryan said.

It was I, George, Mr. James and Mr. Theron was also with us. As usual his phone rang.

"Hello." He answered. "Yes I am not in the office now, please forgive me. No I cannot come now, I have an appointment with Fr. Bryan…yes…no this might take longer, and I will later on confess my sins to him. Okay bye now. See you tomorrow in the morning."

"Please remind me to prepare for your confession later on." Fr. Bryan said.

"No Father, I was just getting rid of that person. I confessed my sins last month, I am fine now." Mr. Theron said.

"But you cannot do that, it is not appropriate to play around with the sacraments of the church. That's a sin on its own. Besides we should all go often to confession so that the Lord forgives our sins even those which we forget."

"Alright, Alright Father. My apologies, I'll remind you later."

"Good! I am Bryan Ehm a Catholic Priest."

"I am Chungu Mumba from Zambia, this is George Eden Bess from Germany."

"Nice to meet you gentlemen. Please feel free to ask anything. These are my parishioners I know them. If I may ask, are you catholic?"

"Yes Fr, very much so."

"Oh I see." He added.

"Mr. Theron told me about you and your research and I was happy to hear about it. Besides you travel all the way from your respective homes just to know more about racism in the States?"

"Yes Fr, that's the only way we can have more knowledge of. Anyway it is better to hear it from the horse's mouth, as they would say. We also did the same in Africa, we went to hear more about the Mfecane wars, that was long time ago."

"You've also been to Africa? Oh my goodness, you're people of interest." He said.

"We've been too many places Fr." George said.

"Fr, as a black and young priest in the early days of these struggles, more especially racism. How did you deal with it, especially As a man of God?" I asked.

"Well Chungu, that's a very good question. But you should've asked first how did we get the vocation to priesthood as blacks. White priests did not believe that Jesus could call black men to priesthood. It was an abomination if you said to a local bishop you would like to join the seminary because you feel like God is calling you to become a priest. At times they would just look at you and laugh sarcastically. Almost all of black men who applied in their Dioceses to join the seminary were rejected, why? Because they are black. Simply black."

"That was very bad Fr." George said.

"Bad, no! That was evil especially from ordained ministers of the church. So to answer your question how did we deal with racism in my early stage as a black priest; you see this started there from the seminaries were we went to be formed as young men who strive to be priests. We were even separated in the institution whites alone blacks alone and even people of color on their own side. Sometimes this took place in the lecture room as well. That side would be for Blacks, that one for people of color and that one for white people. Because we were not that many as blacks and people of color, so we were at times put together as blacks or people of color. Our fellow white seminarians would laugh at us, more especially when we were embarrassed by the lectures and formators in the lecture room or in the institution as a whole. We did not find peace guys, we suffered. We even asked ourselves why did we respond to to this calling. Or did God hate us to such an extent that he handed us over to be clowns of our white brothers. This continued for many years, it did not begin with us, nor ended with us."

"But how cruel was that?" Mr. James said.

"Well we survived until present day. Though we had hope that one day we will become priests to serve the people. We never thought the day of ordination will ever come. Priesthood was never for black people, it was meant for white people.

Some white seminarians felt our pain, many of them had left the seminary because they thought that the treatment which we were given was too much, so the best thing for them was to leave the seminary and try something different. It was not because they did not feel the calling to priesthood anymore, but it was because they couldn't take it anymore. Many of our black seminarians also left the seminary most of them even left the church. It was too much unbearable!"

"Tell us more about your experience as the young priest, or maybe as a black priest." I said.

"That continued until we were ordained, we were glad, very glad to have heard that we were promoted to priesthood. We couldn't believe it, we were very few who survived and that people out there could not believe it either. Our families were overwhelmed with joy as they were praying for us ever since. Although some of them would often ask and advise us to leave the seminary, but they later understood that it was not human who called us to priesthood, but it was God Himself."

"Hmmm."Mr. Theron sighed.

"When at last we were given our parishes, people did not welcome us, because we did not deserve priesthood, it was not for us black people. Black people were overwhelming with joy. Many people even left the church, 'white people' to be more specific. They went to parishes far away from their homes just because their parish priests were black. Those who were with us in the seminary, 'white seminarians' talked to them and they explained that there's no difference between the two. I remember Father Evan Peterson came to my parish one time and had requested that he say Mass that day and I concelebrated in that Mass. In his homily that day, I remember well, he said 'what do you think is special about a white priest? What is it that he has that a black priest doesn't? Whatever I am allowed to do in the church, he also has a right. We are equal. Our ordination is not at all different. But even though, during communion, most people went to receive from Father Evan Peterson."

"Wow!" George said.

"Now what was the role of the Black Panther Party?" I asked.

"Mainly the Black Panther Party was for Self-Defense. African Americans who supported Black Power Movement-believed that use of violence was justified to gain equality for all races. So the Black Panthers as they were known, was established by a men who we known as Huey P Newton, Bobby Seal and Eldridge Cleaver. So it was a group of urban black revolutionaries in Oakland California in October 1966."

"So how active was it Fr?" George asked.

"It was active from the middle 1960's to the end of the 1970's. They wanted full employment, decent housing, black control of the black community and an end to repression and brutality. They had positive intentions, and they fought for blacks, being inspired by the likes of Martin Jr, Malcolm X and even Carmichael."

"What other activities did they do?" They eventually come into conflict with the police. They were also regarded as the "greatest threat" to the internal security of community. Because of these intentions, Stokely Carmichael joined the party, but he did not stay long, he soon left them."

"Why did he leave Fr?" I asked.

"Because they worked with white activists. He was totally against working with white people. He believed that they tended to subvert the black cause. That was his belief."

"What do you thing about that?" I asked.

Father Bryan then looked around, and paused a bit…

"Nothing!" He said.

"Come on Fr. Bryan."

"The Black Panther Party opened the doors for many, restored hope for those who had lost it and had gained confidence to love its people. There was nothing wrong in working with white people who were anti-racists and wanting about change."

"Hmm! The Black Panther Party for Self-Defense." I thought out loud.

"It is recorded that at its inception on October 15 1966, the Black Panther Party's core practice was its armed citizens' patrols to monitor the behavior of officers of the Oakland Police Department including the FBI security. So they challenged the police brutality towards the blacks."

"Did they literally patrol?" George asked.

"George, these people meant business, they were not playing at all. Of course they patrolled literally because they meant their purpose of existence. But it did not end there."

"What else did they do?" I asked.

"The BPP also instituted a variety of community social programs, most extensively the Free Breakfast for Children programs, and community health clinics to address issues like food justice for example. So they enrolled the largest number of members and made the greatest impact in the Oakland-San Francisco Bay area and many other places."

"How nice would it be to have that kind of a political party in our days." Mr. Theron said.

"It would be nice, I must say. A party, which will not only provide food for the people, but a party, which will create, job opportunities for the people. Like the saying 'Don't give a man a fish, but teach him how to fish."

"I like that." Mr. James said.

"So Government oppression initially contributed to the party's growth, as killing and arrests of Panthers increased its support among African Americans and on the broad political left both of whom valued the Panthers as powerful force opposed to de facto segregation and military draft. Like in Church History, when the Emperor Nero and others killed many Christians, they increased in numbers and that is why Tertullian said 'The Blood of the Martyrs is the seed of the church'. That simply meant that every time someone dies for his/her faith they are replaced by multitudes all over the world, and that is why the church is still in existence even today. By 1972, most Panther activity centered on the national headquarters and a school in Oakland, where the party continued to influence local politics."

"Gentlemen, I think that's enough." Mr. James said.

"Well I also have an evening Mass to prepare for." Father Bryan said.

"See you some other time Fr." Mr. Theron said.

"No, you see me now Luke. Please wait for me in the house chapel for your confession."

"I thought we were done with this." Mr. Theron said quietly.

As Fr. Bryan and Mr. Luke were making their own way to the chapel, we remained behind with Mr. Phillip James trying to think where we can go tomorrow for our research.

"Yes! Mr. James said.

"What is it Sir James?" asked George.

"Tomorrow let's meet in bus station, I'll meet you there, at 09h00 O'clock on the dot!" He said.

"Where are we going to?" I asked.

"To Birmingham, to a friend of mine." Sir James said.

"Father says that he's waiting for the next one to go to confess, he still has time before Mass."

"Brothers let us quietly go." Mr. James said making a dash to the door.

We all made a dash to the door, laughing at each other.

CHAPTER FIVE

Students for Democratic Society (USA) & Youth movements (RSA)

We then again woke up early in the morning getting ready to meet Mr. James and Theron in the bus station to Birmingham. We did not know who we were meeting there.

"George stop dawdle it's time to go now."

"Remember the time we were in South Africa, I waited for. It's about time now that you return the favor."

"Whatever Eden."I said.

"We then went to the bus station to meet Mr. James and Theron."

"Right on time gentlemen." Mr. James said.

"Good morning all." Said George.

There was also a sound of a hooter, we then looked around. PARP! PARP! PARP!

Surprisingly it was the priest, Fr. Bryan Ehm.

"Fr, we did not know that you were joining us." Mr. James said.

"I texted Mr. Theron last night to ask where are you planning to go for the next interview because I had few suggestions."

"He did not say anything of that kind to us." Said Mr. James.

"Well, it could be because you did not go to confession yesterday. Besides I was going to share the news with you when the time is right. I mean we just arrived here."

"Whatever Luke." Mr. James said.

"Do you all have the bus tickets with you?"

"Yes Father except yours." Mr. James said

"Here it comes!" I said.

"What?" Asked George.

"The bus." I responded.

"It really feels good to be in the bus again. At least once in a while." Fr. Bryan said.

"I thought you would follow us by your car." George said.

"No George, that's not the proper way. We go with the same transport."

"Who are we meeting again?"

"Michael. Michael Mangisale. We once worked together in Washington DC some time ago. He's a very learned guy."

"Learned like you Luke." James said.

"Did you book an appointment though?" asked Fr. Bryan.

"Don't worry Fr. I don't need to." Mr. James said.

"Amen." Fr said.

"I gave him a hint though, that was last night. All you have to do is to believe in me."

The day was disgustingly hot, very hot! It was like we were in the desert. I remember the cold day on our way to the north east in Lesotho when we were the first students to go there; I just remembered and missed the coldness. In the streets there was an absolute silence as if we were entering a monastery. There was not even a single person in the streets, let alone a car. The houses were very much attracting, nice and big.

"Come he lives in that street. I hope I remember well." Mr. James said.

"You can't hope now, you should be certain. That's all." Mr. Theron said.

"Have faith." He then said.

"You were supposed to be a priest." Fr Bryan said.

"Why Father Ehm." James asked.

"Because you always keep telling us to have faith." Fr responded.

"There he is! Michael...Michael!" Mr. James said.

Mr. James was very happy to see his old friend Michael Mangisale. He was very old though. He had neither beard nor moustache even hair. But what kind of a white man who does not have hair, we used to watch movies like that, not in real life. He was tall, very tall, about two miters. I did not expect to meet a giant like that, maybe not now. His heard was almost abnormal; his hands reached the wrist when he shook my hand. But hey! That was not it that was not all. He was limping. A tall man like him was very much noticeable that there was something wrong with his legs. But hey that was not for me.

"You did not tell me that you were bringing your group with." Mr. Michael said.

"Oh well, I wanted it to be a surprise. That's only if you still like surprises." Mr. James said smilingly.

Michael gave small laughter.

"This is Luke Theron, this is Father Bryan Ehm..."

"A catholic priest?" asked Mr. Mangisale.

"Yes." Fr Bryan responded.

"These two are the reason that we are here. That's George Eden Bess from Germany, and this is Chungu Mumba from Zambia." Mr. James introduced us.

We then told the old tall man the purpose of our visit and the research we have covered already. He was indeed amazed.

"Gentlemen I am impressed, I am speechless. You are people of interest."

"That's what I said to them as well sir." Fr Bryan said.

"What were the causes or what were the student movements of the 1960's and what impact did they have on their societies?" Eden asked.

Whooo! Mr. Michael Mangisale sighed before answering.

"Well, as you would have heard that, the youth and particularly the students were a crucial part of the civil rights movements and even the Black Power Movement. They had learnt valuable lessons in organization and political awareness and to fight for their rights and for others as well."

"Where you part of the student movements sir?" I asked.

"Yes, what's your name again?" Chungu, I replied.

"Yes Chungu, I was part of it. Even my friend Phillip was part of it."

"Which Phillip sir?" George asked.

"This Phillip, Phillip James." He said.

Sir James was smiling as if he was entering the heavens.

"During the mid-1960, 1965-68 round about. The youth revolted, the revolt spread from the inner cities and rural areas, to university campuses across America. Students activists returning from working as volunteers in the civil rights movement or in anti-poverty programmers were more determined and confrontational in their approach to protests against university regulations and later against the Vietnamese War and the draft (conscription)."

"Vietnamese War?" I said.

"Yes, have you heard of it?"

"A little bit." I responded.

"The Vietnamese War also known as the Second Indochina War, and in Vietnam as Resistance War against America or simply the American War was a conflict that occurred in Vietnam, Cambodia and Laos from 1955 to 1975. We may under estimate the power of young people or students if you like, until they take action. Now..." Mr. Michael said and looked around.

"If you happen to be Presidents or Ministers of some sort, make it a point that you listen to young people, don't disappoint them, or else they'll make you a dog by a monkey."

Haha. We all laughed.

"Now, opposition to United States involvement in the Vietnam War began with demonstrations in 1964 against the escalating role of the U.S military in the Vietnam War and grew into a broad social movement over the ensuing several years. This movement also informed and helped shape the vigorous and polarizing debate, primary in the United States, during the second half of the 1960's and early 1970's on how to end the war.

"Are you saying people from the States did not know what was happening in Vietnam?" I asked.

"Not at all Chungu. People did not know that the American Troops were in Vietnam all these years, thanks to the Australian media, who had flown over Vietnam and captured the 'Headlines' of all times."

"That was… I don't know." I said.

"So the youth, students to be more specific, they decided to protest against that. I remember the protests against the Vietnamese War in Washington D.C on 21 October 1967, young people were there. People in America since it was published and known all over the world watched their television, listened to radios and even bought newspapers to be updated. Honestly people did not know about the war, we did not know that our brothers were in Vietnam, killing people, raping women and torturing children because of the frustration of not finding the enemy."

"Yhooo!" George sighed.

"I remember clearly those placards which we raised in those days, 'GET THE HELL OUT OF VIETNAM'… 'NOT IN MY NAME'…'COME BACK HOME'… 'LEAVE THEM IN PEACE' and so on and so forth."

"So the young people made the march to be solid?" George asked.

"It is also recorded in history that, many in the peace movement within the U.S were students and mothers. It also reminds me of the 'French Revolution' the 'March of Bread' to the palace of the King, those were women mostly men and children dressed like women fathers and husbands. Even in Russian Revolution they had a similar thing, were many people died with Fr Gregory Apollonovich Gapon a catholic priest who served the people of God till the last minute of his life. Opposition grew with participation by the African-American civil rights, women's liberation, and Chicano movements, and sectors labor and so on and so forth."

"Oh Michael, you remind me of John Whitehead." Mr. James said.

"Where is he by the way?" Mr. Michael asked.

"Haven't you heard?" Mr. James said.

"Heard what?" asked Mr. Michael.

"That he passed on, his heart gave in!" exclaimed James. "Yes, that was when you were still in Cuba, to finish up your studies."

"I see." Responded Michael. "What was I saying again?" he further asked.

"Please tell us more about the Students for a Democratic Society." Said George.

"SDS as we would call it was a radical student organization. It was the largest and most influential student organization in the USA. SDS worked to correct the problems they found in the American political system by becoming involved in both civil rights movement and the protest movement against the Vietnam War. About 100 000 young people around the States had joined the SDS by 1968. Also student protesters spoke out against corporation and campus administrators. Universities and colleges believed that they were dictatorial and exercised too much control over students. Students on the other hand held rallies and sit-ins to protests restrictions of their rights. Also in 1964 coalition of student groups at the University of California, Barkeley, claimed the right to conduct political activities on campus, the coalition became known as the...."

"Free Speech Movement." Fr. Bryan concluded.

"Thank you Fr Bryan, you still remember it." Said Mr. Michael.

"But there were lot of 'movements' in those days." I said.

Haha. We all laughed after that.

"Wait until you hear this. America was not the only one experiencing the student protests."

"Where else." George asked.

"South Africa. The country you visited."

"We're listening. Sir Michael." I said.

"The Soweto Uprising as it is known, was a series of demonstrations and protests so to speak, led by 'black school children' in South Africa that began on the morning of June 16, 1976."

"Please continue Mr. Mangisale, I'll tell you when to stop." I said.

Mr. Michael gave a small laughter that was followed by the serious face.

"Students from numerous Sowetan schools began to protests in the streets of Soweto in response to the introduction of Afrikaans as the medium of instruction in local schools. It is estimated that about 20 000 students participated in the protests. They were met fierce police brutality. That left about 176 young people killed by police…although estimates count up to about 700 of them left dead."

"That was horrific!" Said Mr. Luke.

"But this 'police brutality!' Exclaimed Mr. James.

"Like in South Africa, it is recorded that discrimination occurred even within the ranks of the police themselves during this time. Many members of the police force even back then were black but no matter the rank of the officer, a white officer outranked them and never had to follow an order given by a black police officer. Also, a black officer could not apprehend any suspect from the white population as well. Considerable energy went into recruiting from the large reservoir of black, Indian, and

Coloured people who viewed law enforcement as a way to move up the socioeconomic ladder though. Despite being given this position of authority, blacks had no real power except among their own populations and the apartheid government's fight against those it deemed terrorists, mainly members of the black population who opposed the policies and practices of apartheid."

For example... Mr. Luke said.

"Members of the African National Congress, ANC, and others who opposed the apartheid government in power were labeled terrorists in a fight to defend South Africa from a wave of communism, which has historically been used by South African governments to wage war on national freedom movements. In the name of battling communism, the police spied on, arrested, interrogated, and eliminated "terrorists" who supported national freedom and a more egalitarian representation in government. However, it is recorded that, the communist threat vanished and it became common knowledge that the threat afterwards was exaggerated in order to maintain the political exclusion of blacks as a way of perpetuating the privileges the National Party enjoyed under the apartheid regime."

"So sir, did the white privileges end to those who were in power?" I asked.

Michael took a moment before responding. "No!" he further said. "The privileges of the white minority did not end with those in office. Afrikaners, as they are identified, in general enjoyed many more rights and benefits than their black and other non-white counterparts. Much of all the crime committed in South Africa occurred in the segregated black townships which left the restrictive white neighborhoods virtually unscathed."

"Was this due to any laws? George asked.

"Very much so George. This was due to influx controls such as pass laws requiring all non-white people to carry a passbook with them at all times which was the only way they would be allowed to be legally present in certain areas of South Africa. From my teacher's perspective, this was resulted, or rather influenced by Charles Darwin's theory of evolution. This was to be considered only to animals and plants, but to a great surprise – to human beings. 'The pass laws protected affluent whites from much of the violence experienced in the townships...when ghetto violence occasionally spilled into white areas, it was quickly pushed back to its source and ignored.' Yet another example of the injustice of apartheid; police action directed at crime instead of perpetuating political power was only directed at stopping crime in Afrikaner neighborhoods but crime such as murder, rape, and robbery were all but ignored within the bounds of the townships. Police forces were given much discretion when it came to combating "terrorists", including forming and employing death squads that would target specific individuals thought to be in opposition to the apartheid regime, but no priority was given to deter crime within black townships."

"A confession from a former police officer during the height of the anti-apartheid movement further proves the existence of death squads"

"So there were confessions after all?" I asked.

"Yes Chungu, even though the apartheid era brought state-operated racism, police brutality, and political killings to a height never seen previously in South Africa, the injustice of apartheid also brought about important changes in accountability for South African police and the government as a whole. Crime did not cease once apartheid legislation was repealed, in fact, the crime rate in South Africa increased. "The murder rate [of South Africa]…is about seven times above that of the United States…rape is reportedly more than three times as common and a lot goes unreported…Robbery occurs at about the same rate as the United States, but carjacking, is notoriously common in urban areas… The police themselves have been reported to be similarly as forceful and trigger-happy as during the reign of apartheid, even here in the States, so both South Africa and America experienced and climbed the same mountain with numerous criminal cases of assault, murder, rape, and sexual assault having been filed against them. In spite of this rise in criminal activity in post-apartheid South Africa, the police forces that have fallen under these charges face actual consequences dissimilar to police under apartheid. They are tried, convicted, and sentenced after any criminal activity like any other criminal. Police may still have a large amount of discretion in how they carry out their duties but now a larger amount of accountability compliments this authority."

"If I get that right, you mean both South Africa and America suffered from the same disease at that time?" I asked.

"Yes, Chungu, both black people in South Africa and in America, felt like they were in the same land. The treatment was the same; there was no difference at all. Not at all! Oh yes I remember, let's go to the neighborhood, we visit each other at least once in a week, every week. She might also contribute to the research."

We then went further down the street, to Mrs. Frans. She was leaving alone like Mr. Masingale, they both lost their spouses with their children studying overseas and some working in far places.

"It happened that our sons be in the same collage in Russia, and they only became friends then, having notice that they were the only ones who were speaking a foreign language. So we too, parents, single parents we decided to befriend each other."

"That's awesome."Said Mr. James said.

"His other son is studying in Rome in the seminary there, I think he is doing his second year Theology if not third."

"Do you know the seminary in Rome Fr?" Mr. Theron.

"Yes, I also completed my Theology there."

"And your Philosophy?"Asked George.

"I did my philosophy here in the States." Fr. Ehm responded. "How do you know that we have to study Philosophy before Theology?" he further asked.

"Well Fr, I also wanted to join the seminary at some point, but many things had happen."

"You mean ladies happen?"

We all laughed at that.

"Well Fr, even before ladies happened, having heard that one needs to do philosophy before theology, and that's about eight and half years, I then decided not to. And then Juliet came to the picture and…"

"… you lost focus." Fr. Ehm concluded.

"It is surprising that I only get to know about these things here and now. They were never shared before, not even in Africa." I said.

"Some of the things Chungu are not meant to be shared." He said.

"I'll take that one."

We then arrived at Mrs. Frans' house. She welcomed us and was happy to see her friend Mr. Michael Masingale, as usual probably. "My day is blessed indeed. What did I do to deserve this visit with a priest among you?" she said.

"Do you know Fr. Bryan?" Asked Mr. Theron.

"Yes I do. I went to his parish a couple of times in the city." She replied.

"The world is so small." Mr. James said.

"Very." Fr. Bryan said.

"If you do not know let me tell, priests are very famous, it's just that they don't realize that, maybe. Working with people could be the reason, we know lot of priests and many of them do not know us, some they do know a lot of people from their own parishes and from other parishes as well, because of their work. Some do know, maybe they forget easily and maybe because of changing parishes affects that. Or maybe the burden is too much on their shoulders "

"We try to remember as many people as we can, but sometimes it is embarrassing when someone greets you with love, zeal and enthusiasm only to find out you can't remember their names, or they are not at all familiar, especially after Mass." Fr. Bryan said shyly.

We might as well sit in the garden; it's cool there. Said Mrs. Frans.

CHAPTER SIX

The Little Rock Nine

Mr. Masingale then introduced us to Mrs. Frans as we were making our way to her beautiful green garden. She was more pink than white, maybe that was caused by the heat. She was short in height but will never notice when sitting down. She had a scar above the left eye, which reminded me of Juliet's. "I am ready for any question gentlemen." She said while gesticulating widely. "I am ready for any question." she said again.

"It is said that Africa is home for all. How true is that?" I asked.

"It is recorded that around 800k BC Ancestors of the Neanderthals and Denisovans left Africa as far back as this time period and replaced or interbred with descendants of Homo erectus. This also can be proven by people like John Reader who are experts in this field."

"So if life began in Africa, then there's nothing like settlers, what's your take on that?" Eden added.

"That's debatable, I must say. But for me, personally I would agree to that philosophy of yours, to some extent though." She said.

"Please tell us about the 'Little Rock Nine'".

"The Little Rock Nine were a group of nine black students who enrolled at formerly all-white Central High School in Little Rock, Arkansas, in September 1957. Their attendance at the school was a test of *Brown v. Board of Education*, a landmark 1954 Supreme Court ruling that declared segregation in public schools unconstitutional. On September 4, 1957, the first day of classes at Central High, Governor Orval Faubus called in the Arkansas National Guard to block the black students' entry into the high school. Later that month, President Dwight D. Eisenhower sent in federal troops to escort the Little Rock Nine into the school. In its Brown v. Board of Education of Topeka decision, issued May 17, 1954, the U.S. Supreme Court ruled that segregation of America's public schools was unconstitutional.

Until the court's decision, many states across the nation had mandatory segregation laws, requiring African-American and white children to attend separate schools. Resistance to the ruling was so widespread that the court issued a second decision in 1955, known as Brown II, ordering school districts to integrate 'with all deliberate speed.'"

"They were brave weren't they?" I said.

"Oh yes indeed." She responded. "In response to the BROWN decisions and pressure from the local chapter of the National Association for the Advancement of Colored People (NAACP), the Little Rock, Arkansas, school board adopted a plan for gradual integration of its schools. The first institutions to integrate would be the high schools, beginning in September 1957. Among these was Little Rock Central High School, which opened in 1927 and was originally called Little Rock Senior High School."

"Wow." Fr. Bryan exclaimed.

"History also records that two pro-segregation groups formed to oppose the plan: the Capital Citizens Council and the Mother's League of Central High School."

"If I follow correctly, in Central High School there were only nine black students." George asked.

"Very much correct George." Mr. James answered.

"Despite the virulent opposition, nine students registered to be the first African Americans to attend Central High School. Minnijean Brown, Elizabeth Eckford, Ernest Green, Thelma Mothershed, Melba Patillo, Gloria Ray, Terrence Roberts, Jefferson Thomas and Carlotta Walls had been recruited by Daisy Gaston Bates, president of the Arkansas NAACP and co-publisher of the Arkansas State Press, an influential African-American newspaper."

"Would you have survived that Mr. Mumba?" George asked.

"I think I would have not. That was between life and death." I said.

"Daisy Bates and others from the Arkansas NAACP carefully vetted the group of students and determined they all possessed the strength and determination to face the resistance they would encounter. In the weeks prior to the start of the new school year, the students participated in intensive counseling sessions guiding them on what to expect once classes began and how to respond to anticipated hostile situations. The group soon became famous as the Little Rock Nine. On September 2, 1957, Governor Orval Faubus announced that he would call in the Arkansas National

Guard to prevent the African-American students' entry to Central High, claiming this action was for the students' own protection. In a televised address, Faubus insisted that violence and bloodshed might break out if black students were allowed to enter the school.

The Mother's League held a sunrise service at the school on September 3 as a protest against integration. But that afternoon, federal judge Richard Davies issued a ruling that desegregation would continue as planned the next day."

CHAPTER SEVEN

The 1983 Constitution and the new dispensation

The draft new constitution set out the new dispensation: a tricameral parliament, a state president with extended powers, and a president's council which effectively had the power to override parliament.

The tricameral parliament was based on a concept of groups with their own racial and cultural identities, and distinguished between general affairs and own affairs, the former affecting all population groups and the latter confined to issues affecting only those groups.

Own affairs would 'affect a population group in relation to the maintenance of its identity and the upholding and furtherance of its way of life, culture, traditions and customs' (Welsh). These included issues related to social welfare, education at all levels, health, community development (including housing), local government (within areas designated for the respective population groups) and agriculture (including financial assistance to farmers).

The parliament would be based on a ratio of Whites to Coloureds and Indians, established at 4:2:1. This translated into 178 White MPs in the House of Assembly, 85 Coloured MPs in the House of Representatives, and 45 Indian MPs in the House of Delegates.

Bills concerned with own affairs needed to be passed only by the House concerned with that particular group, while bills classed as general had to be passed by all three houses. But if these were not passed by the House of Delegates or House of Representatives, the State President had the right to refer the bill to the President's Council, where White MPs had the power to ram the bills through.

The State President, under the new constitution, would have enormous powers. He would appoint 15 members of the President's Council, he would be able to decide which issues were own affairs and which general, he could convene and dissolve parliament, and appoint special committees and Cabinet ministers.

CHAPTER EIGHT

The crises of apartheid in the 1980s

"The question was 'What brought about the crises of apartheid in the 80s?' That was an unanswered question, I remember, even to South Africans who went to exile in Zambia, could not answer it, or maybe they did not want to, unless dealt with."

"Tell us more about the Ku Klux Klan brutality Mrs. Frans.

"Founded in 1866, the Ku Klux Klan (KKK) extended into almost every southern state by 1870 and became a vehicle for white southern resistance to the Republican Party's Reconstruction-era policies aimed at establishing political and economic equality for blacks. Its members waged an underground campaign of intimidation and violence directed at white and black Republican leaders. Though Congress passed legislation designed to curb Klan terrorism, the organization saw its primary goal—the reestablishment of white supremacy—fulfilled through Democratic victories in state legislatures across the South

James Yamkela Qeqe

in the 1870s. After a period of decline, white Protestant nativist groups revived the Klan in the early 20th century, burning crosses and staging rallies, parades and marches denouncing immigrants, Catholics, Jews, blacks and organized labor. The civil rights movement of the 1960s also saw a surge of Ku Klux Klan activity, including bombings of black schools and churches and violence against black and white activists in the South."

"So this Klan originated from of old?" I asked.

"Yes, although they were not known as Ku Klux Klan then, but the doings were very much similar as those who maintained the slave trade and torture toward the blacks."

"Do you want to add something Michael?" asked Mrs. Frans.

"Founding of the Ku Klux Klan." Said Mr. Michael Magisale. "A group including many former Confederate veterans founded the first branch of the Ku Klux Klan as a social club in Pulaski, Tennessee, in 1866. The first two words of the organization's name supposedly derived from the Greek word "kyklos," meaning circle. In the summer of 1867, local branches of the Klan met in a general organizing convention and established what they called an "Invisible Empire of the South." Leading Confederate general Nathan Bedford Forrest was chosen as the first leader, or "grand wizard," of the Klan; he presided over a hierarchy of grand dragons, grand titans and grand cyclopses. At its peak in the 1920s, Klan membership exceeded 4 million people nationwide."

"It was all over the nation?" I asked.

"Yes, they were all over America. They wore white robes and I could not understand why they did that, I don't understand why they put on white robes instead of black. The symbolism of what was totally against what they were doing. I don't know why the Pope did not reprimand them just for wearing white at least."

"That was terrible." Said George.

"So they supported each other, in the work of destroying black people all over the nation. The organization of the Ku Klux Klan coincided with the beginning of the second phase of post-Civil War Reconstruction, put into place by the more radical members of the Republican Party in Congress. So it is recorded that after rejecting President Andrew Johnson's relatively lenient Reconstruction policies, in place from 1865 to 1866, Congress passed the Reconstruction Act over the presidential veto. Under its provisions, the South was divided into five military districts, and each state was required to approve the 14th Amendment, which granted "equal protection" of the Constitution to former slaves and enacted universal male suffrage.

"What about in the South, what really happened."I asked.

"Ku Klux Klan Violence in the South." Mrs. Frans thought before answering.

"From 1867 onward, African-American participation in public life in the South became one of the most radical aspects of Reconstruction, as blacks won election to southern state governments and even to the U.S. Congress. For its part, the Ku Klux Klan dedicated itself to an underground campaign of violence against Republican leaders and voters (both black and white) in an effort to reverse the policies of Radical Reconstruction and restore white supremacy in the South. They were joined in this struggle by similar organizations such as the Knights of the White Camelia (launched in Louisiana in 1867) and the White Brotherhood. At least 10 percent of the black legislators elected during the 1867-1868 constitutional conventions became victims of violence during Reconstruction, including seven who were killed. White Republicans (derided as "carpetbaggers" and "scalawags") and black institutions such as schools and churches—symbols of black autonomy—were also targets for Klan attacks.

By 1870, the Ku Klux Klan had branches in nearly every southern state. Even at its height, the Klan did not boast a well-organized structure or clear leadership. Local Klan members–often wearing masks and dressed in the organization's signature long white robes and hoods–usually carried out their attacks at night, acting on their own but in support of the common goals of defeating Radical Reconstruction and restoring white supremacy in the South. Klan activity flourished particularly in the regions of the South where blacks were a minority or a small majority of the population, and was relatively limited in others. Among the most notorious zones of Klan activity was South Carolina, where in January 1871 500 masked men attacked the Union county jail and lynched eight black prisoners."

"That was not easy." Fr. Bryan said.

"Not at all." Mr. James added.

"Though Democratic leaders would later attribute Ku Klux Klan violence to poorer southern whites, the organization's membership crossed class lines, from small farmers and laborers to planters, lawyers, merchants, physicians and ministers. In the regions where most Klan activity took place, local law enforcement officials either belonged to the Klan or declined to take action against it, and even those who arrested accused Klansmen found it difficult to find witnesses willing to testify against them.

Other leading white citizens in the South declined to speak out against the group's actions, giving them tacit approval. After 1870, Republican state governments in the South turned to Congress for help, resulting in the passage of three Enforcement Acts, the strongest of which was the Ku Klux Klan Act of 1871.

For the first time, the Ku Klux Klan Act designated certain crimes committed by individuals as federal offenses, including conspiracies to deprive citizens of the right to hold office, serve on juries and enjoy the equal protection of the law. The act authorized the president to suspend the writ of habeas corpus and arrest accused individuals without charge, and to send federal forces to suppress Klan violence. This expansion of federal authority–which Ulysses S. Grant promptly used in 1871 to crush Klan activity in South Carolina and other areas of the South–outraged Democrats and even alarmed many Republicans. From the early 1870s onward, white supremacy gradually reasserted its hold on the South as support for Reconstruction waned; by the end of 1876, the entire South was under Democratic control once again.

In 1915, white Protestant nativists organized a revival of the Ku Klux Klan near Atlanta, Georgia, inspired by their romantic view of the Old South as well as Thomas Dixon's 1905 book "The Clansman" and D.W. Griffith's 1915 film "Birth of a Nation." This second generation of the Klan was not only anti-black but also took a stand against Roman Catholics, Jews, foreigners and organized labor. It was fueled by growing hostility to the surge in immigration that America experienced in the early 20th century along with fears of communist revolution akin to the Bolshevik triumph in Russia in 1917. The organization took as its symbol a burning cross and held rallies, parades and marches around the country. At its peak in the 1920s, Klan membership exceeded 4 million people nationwide.

The Great Depression in the 1930s depleted the Klan's membership ranks, and the organization temporarily disbanded in 1944. The civil rights movement of the 1960s saw a surge of local Klan activity across the South, including the bombings, beatings and shootings of black and white activists. These actions, carried out in secret but apparently the work of local Klansmen, outraged the nation and helped win support for the civil rights cause. In 1965, President Lyndon Johnson delivered a speech publicly condemning the Klan and announcing the arrest of four Klansmen in connection with the murder of a white female civil rights worker in Alabama. The cases of Klan-related violence became more isolated in the decades to come, though fragmented groups became aligned with neo-Nazi or other right-wing extremist organizations from the 1970s onward. In the early 1990s, the Klan was estimated to have between 6,000 and 10,000 active members, mostly in the Deep South."

"Please tell them about the 1956 Women's March in Pretoria, South Africa." Said Mr. Luke Theron.

"The power of women. That's what I call it." She said.

Everybody was staring at Mrs. Frans.

"Not because I am a woman." She defended.

We all laughed.

"Any way, you men are jealous. The 1956 Women's March in Pretoria, South Africa constitutes an especially noteworthy moment in women's history. On 9 August 1956, thousands of South Africa women – ranging from all backgrounds and cultures including Indians, Colored, Whites, and Blacks – staged a march on the Union Buildings of Pretoria to protest against the abusive pass laws. Estimates of over 20,000 women – some carrying young children on their backs, some wearing traditional dresses and sarees, and others clothed in their domestic work outfits – all showed up to take part in the resistance against apartheid. The 1956 Women's March played a vital role in the women becoming more visible participants in the apartheid struggle.

In South Africa, pass laws were a form of an internal passport system designed to segregate the population between Blacks from Whites in South Africa, and thereby, severely limit the movements of the black African populace, manage urbanization, and allot migrant labor. As early as 1893, pass laws originated in the capital of the Orange Free State of South Africa, Bloemfontein, requiring non-white women and men to carry documentation to validate their whereabouts. Pass laws were a means of trying to control South Africans of getting into the city, finding better work, and establishing themselves in the "white" part of town, which of course was desirable on account of employment opportunities and transportation. If non-Whites sought to enter the restricted areas destitute of their passes, they suffered imprisonment and worse. In 1912 the Free State women managed to collect five thousand signatures in protest against women passes. A delegation of six women presented their case to the Minister of Native Affairs, H. Burton, in which he responded that in the future "he would take action to eliminate pass regulations." (Wells) A year later when no changes were made, women found their frustrations growing as the government continued to ignore their demands. On 29 March 1913, women "pledged to refuse to carry passes any longer and expressed their willingness to endure imprisonment." (Wells) The escalation of pass laws continued and triggered growing irritation."

"Let's call it a day gents." Mr. Theron said.

"Let's have something to toothsome."

We then enjoyed the meal, prepared by Mrs. Frans. That meal, from that moment seeing everyone laughing, it quickly reminded me of our last meal in Lesotho in the royal house. Yes that one!

"We better get going before we miss the buy." Sir. James said.

"Yes, thank you so much Mrs. Frans, we really appreciate your input." Said Luke.

"Please Fr. Before you leave, will you kindly bless me?" pleaded Mrs. Frans.

"Bless us all Fr. Please." Added Mr. Michael.

Fr. Bryan then said the blessing.

P "I raise my eyes to the mountains."

R "Where my help comes from."

P "Our help is in the name of the Lord."

R "Who made heaven and earth."

P "The Lord be with you."

R "And with your spirit."

P "May the almighty God, bless and protect you in the name of the Father + Son and the Holy Spirit."

R "Amen."

"Thank you for the day everyone. Especially you Mrs. Frans and Mr. Mangisale." Fr. Bryan said.

We then went to the bus stop, to catch the bus to the city.

"What would you do if your car is stolen Fr." Sir. James said.

"Don't talk like that James." Besides that car has a Holy Rosary.

"I hear you." He said.

The bus came and we traveled to the city. Praying the Rosary together. After a while, we then arrived in the bus station.

"You see there's my car still safe." Fr. Bryan said.

CHAPTER NINE

The Women's movement in Action.

"Where are we going tomorrow?" Mr. James asked.

"Let's go to Paul." He said.

"Paul who?" Mr. Theron asked.

"Gantson. Paul Gantson." He replied.

"It would be appropriate then to book an appointment with him before we barge in."

"Don't worry about that."

When we got to our apartment, it was when I realized how much I miss my beloved family. Sometimes we may take our families for granted and that we don't feel any closeness when we're with them. But believe me you, when we're away we feel their space in our lives. Sometimes I feel pity for people like Fr. Bryan (Catholic priests) so to speak, I always wonder how do they cope without a family. Yes they all have families, but I mean their own families. To me that's the most highest sacrifice that a human being can make. We do underestimate other people's sacrifices at times, and we take every vocation for granted.

"What are you thinking about Chungu?" George asked.

"Nothing my friend, nothing serious at least." I said.

"Well you better take your position and stand by the stove, because we are not eating take aways tonight." George said.

"You are an interesting person George. The last time I checked I was the last one to stand on the stove, and I sweated like nobody's business. I think you should make yourself useful and stand there yourself."

"But my friend you know that you're good in the kitchen. Why don't you groom your talent and make a best out of it. I mean if you don't cook God may take away that talent and give it to someone else who will use it and make best out of it."

"George, if you try to impress me, you should do better than that." I said.

"Alright! Alright! Chungu." He said. "Will you please cook for us…please…? You are the best in the kitchen my friend, you don't want a stomachache do you?"

"Oh well, you have a point there. Immediately when you see a steam coming out the food is ready to you."

"Haha." George laughed.

"Do you still remember the food prepared by Ma Makutsho while we were still in Lesotho?" He asked.

"How can I forget that divine meal, cooked with love and zeal?"

"You should make something similar to that. I love African food."

"You should remember that we're in the States, not in Africa. You'll eat African food when you're in Africa. I don't want to be investigated by the FBI."

We both gave a laugh on that. Anyway, another night went by, we were ready to meet the man called Paul Gantson.

Parp! Parp!

Fr. Bryan's car was waiting for us outside the apartment.

"Chungu, come let's go. Fr. Bryan and the team is waiting for us outside." George said.

It was also at that moment when I realized that, we were now a team of researchers and that we had a great motivation for each other. That was one of the most interesting part of that research in the United States of America."

"Come on now guys, let's go!" Sir James shouted."

"Here we are Sir James. We may go now." I said.

"Sorry about that gentlemen, someone doesn't know how to manage his time." George said.

"Good morning Chungu and George." Mr. Theron said from the front seat."

"Good morning, Good morning everyone. Sorry we're late." I said.

"You must work on your time management guys. I know it can be tough, but you should try it anyway." Fr. Bryan said.

"Yes, you should work on that gentlemen." Mr. Theron added.

"You know, no one wants to be rich, everyone wants to have money and by having money we get more choices. The more we get money the more choices we have. So everyone wants to have a better choice.

"What is to be rich then according to you?"

"Is to have everything in life, which is still impossible."

We then arrived at Mr. Paul's house. It was a big wooden house, kind of. It was nicely built, a mixture of wood and bricks. It was really beautiful. Mr. Paul was playing a piano, his son was blowing the lute while the wife was dancing with her other son, the daughter was singing one of the their composed songs. It was an amazing family.

"So welcome to this singing family gentlemen." Mr. Paul said smiling.

"Thank you Paul, thanks a lot." Sir James said.

We then introduced ourselves to Mr. Paul.

"So, what brings you here?" Paul asked.

"These young gentlemen are doing a research on African American and the treatment of blacks around the world. The link between the South Africa's and America's struggle. Basically now, they would like to learn more on the role played by women in both states." Mr. Luke said.

"So you are part of the research Luke?" Mr. Paul asked.

"Well you can say that Paul, it looks like that though." He responded.

"So let me begin." Paul said. "In 1955." He continued. "Government officials in the Orange Free State declared that women living in the urban townships would be required to buy new entry permits each month. In response to the government's request, South African women decided to petition and create a document of their values in "The Demand of the Women of South Africa for the Withdrawal of Passes for Women and the Repeal of the Pass Laws," a document which was presented to the Prime Minister. It demanded that the government terminate pass laws. Unified they stood in saying *once the women have made up their minds that they will do it, the women will organize and fight, and you will never stop them.*" The petition exemplified their frustration with the government. They were tired of seeing their families "suffering under the bitterest law of all

- the pass law which has brought untold suffering to every African family." (ANC) The petition clearly exemplified their indignation towards the government's stance on pass laws. Women were tired of the government insisting that the pass laws were abolished, but it is the wives, mothers, and "women that know this is not true, for [their] husbands, [their] brothers, and [their] sons are still being arrested, thousands every day, under these very pass laws." (ANC) During that time "the husband would come to the house and tell his wife, *"I'm going to jail now."*

"Oh! My goodness." I said.

"And what would the wife say?" George asked.

"And then the wife would say, *'Well, I'm going to jail too.'* A good example would be President Nelson Mandela and his wife Mama Winnie Madikizela Mandela, and many others as well, people like Mr. Robert Sobukhwe and Mama Victoria Sobukhwe. Their formidable courage exhibited the absence of gender roles in the sense of dominating activist ideals. Previously, men would often voice the opinions of the household, willing to take the consequences, but with the rise and works of the 1956 Women's March, women were eager and ready for every and any repercussions.

By the way, Mr. Paul was originally from South Africa, who had lived in the States for about forty years. He had moved to the States because he thought that things were better there in terms of racism and segregation. He had been married to Nervita since those years of apartheid in South Africa.

"So what about the rise to political prominence of women Mr. Paul." I asked.

"That's a very good and important question Chungu." He said." "Perhaps in retrospect, the rise to political prominence of women was inevitable given that they arguably possessed acute senses as to the destructive repercussions that the pass laws imposed upon families. Women thoroughly comprehended the destruction and detrimental services that the pass laws served within the dynamics of the family setting. The women of South Africa started to realize the tearing away of their family due to the pass laws: it was confining the man, inherent to embrace freedom in his own land, while also destroying the gentle aura, yet protective presence of the motherly woman. With the addition of pass laws, the typical person could not feel as if they were truly inhibiting their character when pushed amongst a wall of confinement and complete control, of course mixed with the ever-so-present ubiquity of apartheid."

"And the pass laws Mr. Paul." George said.

"In laying out what the pass laws meant to them, the women of South Africa further explained *that homes will be broken up when women are arrested under pass laws.*' (ANC) With their frustrations high and their immense dedication, the women of South Africa promised that they "shall not rest until ALL pass laws and all forms of permits restricting our freedom have been abolished" and "shall not rest until we have won for our children their fundamental rights of freedom, justice, and security." (ANC) The immense amount of passion and determination to make a change is what brought these women together to make history and show the important role of women engaging in activism. These activists "were a big force," and according to Dorothy Masenya, one of the many women who participated in the 1956 March, no one could stop them – "if they arrest one we all walk in [to jail] and no turning back." (SAHO-women's interviews) The women realized that there is strength and power in numbers; that together they can make a difference, and that the government might struggle to stop a unit. The participants accepted significant risks such as arrest or imprisonment, in order to pursue their goal."

"Well of course when I moved to the States, Nervita was the first person I met, in the marches of Mississippi and in other places. I fell in love with her, just like that. I went to her one time, she asked where I was from, I told her, that I was running away from the struggles in South Africa. After telling her that she just laughed and I was surprised how can somebody laugh at another's problem."

We laughed after hearing that.

"But what did you tell her after that?"

"I did not say anything, but she just folded her face and said with a sarcastic voice, 'welcome to the struggle.'"

"Indeed I was in the struggle."

"There was a time when you went back to South Africa, is that correct?" Mr. Luke said.

"Yes, that's correct." He responded.

"Then what brought you back?" asked Luke again.

"People like John Kani, Miriam Makheba also known as 'Mama Africa' made me to realize that it was not going to help to run away from the struggle, more especially when other people were suffering for their country. My wife also Nevirta, encouraged me to go back and fight for freedom. But then it was not easy because she had already been married to me and that we had our first born to take care. So I would go and come, I was not so kin to go back, I did not want to die in the struggle, I did not want my son to grow up not knowing me."

"It make sense." Fr. Bryan said.

Their unified determination established their role in the anti-resistance movement with their use of media, particularly in songs and in photographs. The photograph "Women's March", taken by Peter Magubane the day of the march, clearly depicts the unification and strength of women across the country. Several women have their right arm raised high with a clenched fist, a common symbol of power. Whilst marching, the women of the 1956 march sang the now infamous 'Wathint' abafazi Strijdom, wathint' imbokodo, uza kufa", translated, "you strike the women Strijdom you strike a rock, you will be crushed, you will die" The song was repeatedly sang and dispersed as their freedom anthem amongst the city, in hopes it would echo across the country. The amalgam of women further exhibits the unifying ideals of the feminist empowerment and movement distributed through South Africa in hopes of diminishing pass laws."

By the way, Nevirta was just with us in the room, listening attentively.

"I tend to forget some of the things." Paul said.

"What about the influential actors in the conception of the 1956 women's march ma'am?" I asked.

"Good question." Nevirta said. "Influential actors in the conception of the 1956 women's march. The march also made several female leaders visible in the struggle against apartheid, particularly Lilian Ngoyi and Helen Joseph. There cannot be change and reconstruction without leaders who are willing to run risks, making a lasting effect. Leaders such as Lilian Ngoyi and Helen Joseph were essential to the brainstorming, organization, and execution of the remarkable event of the 1956 Women's March."

James Yamkela Qeqe

"We are listening attentively Ma'am."

"In the beginning stages, A historian notes very well that, Mama Lillian Ngoyi went around addressing meetings and rallies all over the country; she called on women to be in the forefront of the struggle, in order to secure a better future for [their] children. Lillian Ngoyi joined the African National Congress (ANC) in 1952, along with political pioneers Kate Mxaktho, Ida Mtwana and Charlotte Mxeke, who co-founded the Women's League within the ANC. Ngyoi advised that "only direct mass action will deter the Government and stop it from proceeding with its cruel laws." (Brooks, 223) With that being said, Lilian Ngoyi, as well as other influential leaders, led 20,000 women to protest the inclusion of women in the pass laws controlling the movements of blacks. Holding thousands of petitions in one hand, Lilian Ngoyi personally knocked on Prime Minister J.G. Strijdom's door to give him the petitions. Lilian Ngoyi did not stop her work in Africa, she soon realized and "recognized the potential influence that international support could have on the struggle against apartheid and the emancipation of black women." (Grant) Lilian realized that she needed global support from women of diverse backgrounds in order to strengthen freedom and democracy in South Africa. As the National Chairman of the Federation of South African Women (FEDSAW), Ngoyi questioned her audience as to why they "have heard of men shaking in their trousers, but who ever heard of a woman shaking in her skirt?" at the inaugural conference. (Grant) Ngoyi's several positions in leadership have led her to be one of the strongest, black women in politics of South Africa. Because of her great efforts and intense involvement with the ANC and the liberation movement, Ngoyi was arrested and tried for treason; despite that, she remained outspoken on issues regarding Africans and women."

"Are there any other influential women apart from these which you have mentioned?" George asked.

"Another influential woman was Helen Joseph, a white anti-apartheid activist. Though there were few white activist against apartheid, Helen Joseph believed that they 'shall not rest until the pass laws and all forms of permits restricting our freedom has been abolished.' Helen Joseph, though a white woman, believed it was intolerant to watch the suffrage and separation of South Africa due to pass laws. As part of the Women's League in the African National Congress she noted that, "she was not a woman doing things for black people but a member of a mixed committee headed by lack women." Helen Joseph's values were those of justice and fair treatment, race or color was not a factor in her involvement to a better South Africa. When joining the movement, she "looked at those many faces until they became only one face, the face of suffering black people." (Joseph, 5) The images of those whose land and freedom have been taken away from them inspired Joseph to make a difference.

The Broader Significance of the 1956 Women's March

"The legacies of the 1956 Women's March include the rise of several strong female leaders, now visible in the greater struggle against apartheid, as well as the presence of women in mass media that called upon the march to inspire others. Helen Joseph mentions that 'it is a story that continues every day.' The women of South Africa joined in forces all for one cause, showing the immense amount of unification and influence that women have in wanting to make a vital change in the entire continent. Several different groups inclined toward fostering women's empowerment about within the same time period as the initiation of women's involvement in resistance politics."

"The power of women." I said.

"Say that I gain, without the force of frustrated and determined women, South Africa's anti-apartheid resistance may not have been abolished without the assistance of women. During the march, the women sang "WATHINT' ABAFAZI, WATHINT' IMBOKODO, UZA KUFA! – TRANSLATING THAT [WHEN] YOU STRIKE THE WOMEN, YOU STRIKE A ROCK, YOU WILL BE CRUSHED [YOU WILL DIE]! The phrase is "SO POWERFUL THAT IT HAS LOCKED INTO OUR MINDS." It is constantly repeated to remind the historic moment when "WOMAN MANAGED TO CREATE A PUBLIC VOICE FOR THEMSELVES." The song represented their courage, strength, and confidence that there will be changes and an end to the pass laws. The song is still recalled today, over the several years after the abandonment of pass laws. South Africans continue to remember the song in tribute of the power that women had. They constantly refer to themselves as a rock to symbolize themselves as a weapon to be feared.

Additionally, one of the most common images of this movement was reproduced in posters such as that shown below, entitled: "Now that you have touched the women, you have a struck a rock, you have dislodged a boulder, you will be crushed." The poster was re-created by Judy Seidman, an artist in the Medu Art Ensemble in Botswana, South Africa. Dated in 1981, the poster shows that even after 25 years, the march was still being called upon. The poster shows a black woman with a strong, stout face raising her right arm, which has a broken chain on her wrist."

"So Seidman's poster," Paul said. Reflects the strength, tenacity, and frustration that the South African woman faced, clearly seen by the expressions on her face. The image shows the revelation and freedom that women commanded in order to repeal the pass laws. In some cases, the women further established that "once you have touched the women, you are going to die" further establishing their prevalence in the means of the death of the pass laws. The poster highlighted the anthem of the anti-apartheid women struggle. When women come together for a bigger cause, a cause that affects their very kin and being, they find strength within each other to further push them towards the goal. In an era when black women did not and –in some cases, could not have a voice, the woman of South Africa shouted, screamed, and yelled in order to get what they rightly deserved, freedom. The involvement of women in activist pursuits has become an authoritative historical point.

The significance of this march still reigns today in South Africa's annual celebration of National Women's Day in regards and respect to that very day 58 years ago on August 9th. The peacefully aggressive nature characterized the women's march: they did not stop until pass laws were repealed, but they never used violence to progress in their movement. This event illustrated the strength, determination and power that women possess when come across a situation that puts fear of the wellbeing of their children's future and their kin. In an era where women's voices were not always heard, the women of South Africa demanded attention for their freedom."

"Let me share a presentation of one priest on Racism some time ago." Said Paul.

"The past is not so far distant because we still experience the past even in our days." Fr Bryan Massingale an American priest opened the Winter Living Theological School with these words. He introduced three stages with which we would focus on, through the course of the winter schools, 1. See; 2. Judge and 3. Act. On the first day he took us through the 'See' stage, that we need to see the problem, and recognize it. Seeing the problem, is to comprehend the situation and to be mindful of the circumstances in this case 'racism'. "Racism is the problem, but not thee problem," he further said. Fr Bryan made us attendees to be aware of it and to actually do something about it, before it does something about us. At times we fall to the temptation of thinking that racism comes from one group to the other. But through his presentation, he explained that it actually comes from all races and that it affects all races. We can also say all races are racist but some races are more racists than others, which sound like the seventh commandment in the book 'Animal Farm' "All animals are equal, but some animals are more equal than others."

Nevertheless, in the reflection questions Fr. Bryan assisted us to discover that "Racism is a culture."It can be adopted, it can be learnt, and it can be practiced. Racism is all over, and that it will never end unless we do something about it. In some cases people are aware of it, but in some cases people are not aware of it. This could be on purpose that people are aware of it, but turn a blind eye to it. For example, when Adolph Hitler was asked to describe a black person, he said 'Black people are the freak of nature'. In simple terms he himself believed that there was something better being created but then occurred a mistake and a black person appeared from that which was a mistake. So now tell me, if Hitler was that kind of a person, what would make his followers different from him? Bishop Dabula Mpako of Queenstown was asked to give his reflection. He described racism as "The core of racism is the belief in white superiority of the system."

The second stage was, to 'judge' 4th July. Now that we have seen the problem, how do we judge it? In this stage, we learn that we must look and reflect on oneself first, because at times we have a tendency of judging other people without looking where we lack. Like the Gospel "You hypocrite, first take the plank out of your own eye, and then you will see clearly to remove the speck from your brother's eye." (Mt 7:5).

On the last day 5th July we were closely drawn to the last stage which is 'Act'. Now that we have seen, and judged, now it's time to act. I asked a question to Fr. Bryan, that how to exorcise these demons of racism, xenophobia, segregation, sexism and even tribalism. Fr. Bryan gave a simple answer, which made a lot of sense. That 'Jesus the Lord, commanded us to name the demon when exorcising it.' So it is appropriate to name the demon as it is, and that we the community we talk about it, Black or White, Indian or Colored. We are one, one we are. The question is 'where to from here?' Truly I say: we cannot heal the past, unless we retell the story.

"Please give us a little bit of background of the apartheid in South Africa Mr. Paul." I said.

"From 1948 to early 1990s South Africa practiced a policy of racial separation and inequality called apartheid. The white minority dominated and oppressed the black majority. The government used brute force to maintain this policy."

"Ouch!" Fr. Bryan said.

"Resistance to apartheid intensified after the 1976 June 16 Uprising. There was political unrest in the country, worse enough in the eighties the political unrest made the apartheid state ungovernable-almost a state of insurrection. Also the government's response was to declare successive states of emergency. So in 1986 a national state of emergency was declared. Curfews were imposed, political funerals, meetings restricted, news censorship became common. And indeed the country was literally burning."

"That was tough wasn't Mr. Paul?" I asked.

"Tough is understatement, it was hell!" he said.

At that moment came the youngest daughter of Paul bringing some refreshments. Also came good friend of Paul, Peter.

"Welcome Peter." Said Paul.

"I can come some other time, I did not know that you had visitors." Said Peter.

"Your input would be much appreciated Peter."

Paul then explained the purpose of our visit.

"I see, Peter said, with a smile."

We then in the same manner introduced ourselves to Mr. Peter.

"Let's talk about the contradictions of apartheid." He said.

"That's sounds interesting." Sir James said.

"By the 1970s it became clear that apartheid was holding back the economic development of South Africa. Inherent contradictions within apartheid became apparent. Grand Apartheid was no longer workable, but the denial was at ease. Also the homeland system was not working, or maybe no longer working. The homelands were economically dependent on South Africa and were not recognized internationally. Cities needed African workers but the presence of Africans in cities was restricted by pass laws, influx control law and so on and so forth. "

"Mr. Peter, why did the cities need African workers, is it because they were the majority?" I asked.

"That's the best answer you just gave. Exactly it was because the whites were so few that they could not do everything by themselves, they needed us to partake in the factories and even in the mines."

By the way, Peter was also a South African by birth, and had moved to work in the States after the first elections.

"South Africa did not have enough skilled workers to support a growing economy. It became difficult to police pass laws in the eighties as millions of Africans defied pass laws and entered urban centers. The pass laws introduced in 1952 were repealed in 1986, they were no longer valid in one sense."

"We are still listening Mr. Peter." Said Fr. Bryan.

"In 1977 the government appointed Wiehahn Commission recommended that Africans be permitted to join trade unions."

"What would that mean?" Fr. Bryan asked.

"This would allow government to control and regulate the growing union movement. In 1979 the Labor Relations

Act legalized black trade unions. Trade unions became an important element in the anti-apartheid struggle. Government could not control them. Union's leaders played an important role in community organizations. Also in 1985 the **C**ongress **O**f **S**outh **A**frican **T**rade **U**nion was formed, what later became known as the COSATU."

"Oh, I see. So that was in 1985 when it came to existence." I asked.

"Yes, sir. So another contradiction was that the South Africa's economy was dependent on cheap black migrant labour. But the labour environment was antagonistic towards African workers."

"How evil!" Fr. Bryan commented.

"It was evil indeed Father Bryan. It was suffering after suffering, pain after pain, agony after agony, scourging after scourging. We regretted the day we first saw the sun."

"If you may Mr. Peter, tell us about P.W. Botha's total strategy- the Tri-cameral Parliament." I pleaded.

"You are very much observant, what's your name again?"

"Chungu." I responded.

"Yes, Chungu, Pieter Willem Botha was the Prime Minister of South Africa and he wanted a strategy to weaken and isolate the liberation movement. A new constitution was adopted in 1983."

"Are you saying Botha introduced the Tri-Cameral Parliament in 1983." George asked.

"Exactly! We are together. But also there were objectives to the Tri-Cameral Parliament."

"Please share with us Mr. Peter." I said.

"To introduce a measure of power sharing while the white minority retained real power. That was one objective to it."

"Okay…" I said.

"The second one was to weaken the liberation movement-through dividing the oppressed majority."

"I am following." George said."

"The third objective was to deceive the world into believing that there was inclusive political governance in South Africa."

"Please explain the term Tri-Cameral Parliament to us Mr. Peter." Said Fr. Bryan.

"Parliament to consist of three houses (Tri-Cameral) the House of Assembly for whites, House of Delegates for Indians and the House of Representatives for coloureds."

"You have answered me Peter." Responded Bryan.

"But what about the 'Africans', or the natives…where were they expected to practice their political rights, since they were not included in the Tri-Cameral Parliament?" Asked George.

"I like that question George. Your mind clicks fast. But I'll answer that later on. The functions of government were categorized into two broad categories- 'general affairs' and 'own affairs'. The House of Assembly remained the house of final instance, as it had to approve laws made by the other houses. So the answer to your question George, the Africans were expected to exercise their political rights in the homelands."

"Where there any response the Tri-Cameral Parliament?" I asked.

"Very much so, a number of responses for that matter. In response to the Parliament, the United Democratic Front was formed. The UDF as it was known, it was an umbrella organization for all organizations that were against the 1983 Constitution and apartheid in general."

"It was a mother organization you meant?" I asked.

"Yes, Chungu, it was a mother body of all the organizations. Also the UDF co-ordinated the struggles of different sectors in the country such as civil organizations, schools, churches, trade unions, women's organization, and university students into what became called the Mass Democratic Movement. Not as 'Mass' as you would understand Father Bryan."

We all gave a laugh to that.

"So that was the UDF." Said Peter.

"What about the 'Internal Resistance' to Botha's reforms, where there any?" Asked Mr. Luke.

"Of course there were some internal resistance so to speak. After 1976 trade unions began to play a major role in the struggle. The workers demanded political rights as part of their programmes. It was understood that the national question had to be addressed sooner than later. In 1979, 12 small unions form the **F**ederation **O**f **S**outh **A**frican **T**rade Union."

"That's what became known as FOSATU right?" Asked Sir James.

"FOSATU, correctly so." Peter said. "FOSATU", Peter continued. Did not align itself with any of the liberation movements and that was the best decision it ever taken as my history teacher would say Mr. Chris Hubert Nenzani, 'That was the very best decision, ever!' In 1985 COSATU was formed and it aligned itself with the African National Congress. Elijah Barayi was its first president with Jay Naidoo as General Secretary. The trade union movement became the voice of the oppressed majority. Communities led by the UDF as part of the Mass Democratic Movement rejected Botha's reforms."

"This is very interesting." I said.

"Now, Botha's reforms were cosmetic changes with the apartheid policy still firmly in place. Blacks still did not vote, also the demand for the destruction of apartheid became more profound."

"Did the students play a role in that?" Fr. Bryan asked.

"Fr Bryan, one thing you must know, that students are very powerful in our history. And we owe it also to them. Black students led by the Congress Of South African Students, COSAS in short, adopted a slogan that said, "Liberation before Education."But to me that was not the best at all, I don't know, but education is still number one to me."

"I agree with you there Peter!" said Luke.

"But hey let's keep in to ourselves, I would sound like a 'sellout' to my brethren. So black councilors in townships and others who collaborated with the apartheid state were killed. Like the 'Necklace' method of killing became common."

"What method was that?" I asked George.

"That was a method were they put a tire around your neck with fuel on it and burn it eventually." Responded Peter.

"Ouch!" George said.

"So a number of things became common, like the entrance to townships were barricaded to keep police out. Mass mobilization became a key strategy against the state, funerals also on the other hand were a key mobilization platform."

"Tell us more Peter." Paul said.

"Civil organizations played an active role in mobilizing communities against apartheid, churches and religious groups joined forces with the oppressed people to fight against apartheid. Church leaders also played a crucial role, people like the Anglican Archbishop Desmond Tutu, Dr.

Frank Chikane, Dr. Alan Boesak, Dr. Beyers Naude and many more, they became prominent anti-apartheid leaders. The South African Council of Churches supported non-violent actions to fight against apartheid, which sounds like Dr. Martin Luther King Jr."

"Exactly my point Sir, in a way in this research we are linking the two struggles, of the apartheid and of Civil Rights." I said.

"Well there's a lot in common between the two. That's why my wife said to me 'welcome to the struggle." Said Paul.

"That's true, there's a lot in common, we are not at all different, but what we need to do is to tell the true African history." Peter said.

"You sound like the great Kamala now." I said.

"Who's that now?" asked Peter.

"The other old man we met in Southern Africa, just after World War II." George answered.

"So you've been there?" asked Peter again.

"Oh yes! Many years ago, when we were still students." I said.

"We were doing a research on the Mfecane War, fighting Xenophobia."

"I admire you young men, now you're fighting racism." Mr. Peter. "Where were we again?" he further asked." UDF co-ordinated the 'Don't Vote Campaign' against the Tri-Cameral elections."

"How is this possible, did the House of Assembly want the natives to vote while they were excluded in the Tri-Cameral?" I asked.

"Surprising enough, yes they did expect them to. So the UDF was affiliated to the ANC and it adopted the Freedom

Charter as its guiding document. Opposition to the Tri-Cameral Parliament united the Masses of South Africa. So also in 1988 the government restricted the UDF and COSATU."

"What!" exclaimed George.

"Yes George. The Mass Democratic Movement coordinated resistance activities. The MDM was not a single organization but a loose alliance of many organizations."

"What is the MDM Mr. Peter? I think I am left out now."

"It's Mass Democratic Movement in abbreviation George. I said.

"Oh sorry, you may continue Mr. Peter." He then said.

"Now the MDM organized a gathering in 1989, a gathering of all anti-apartheid structures inside South Africa in what became known as the Conference for a Democratic Future in Nasrec, Johannesburg. So the MDM organized marches throughout South Africa and the flags of the ANC and SACP were regular features at these marches. Another blow for the state was End Conscription Campaign the ECC. White youths refused to enlist for the army as it had been the norm under the compulsory military conscription policy of the state. Now the ECC...."

"The ECC stands for End Conscription Campaign George." I said.

"I know Chungu." He said.

"In 1999 ECC was banned by the state, white conscientious objectives were rallied the view that 'apartheid was not worth dying for.' Another white organization that fought against the apartheid policy was the Black Sash."

"The Black Sash." Fr Bryan said."

"Yes Father, it was a kind of a 'Diaconate stole' which comes over one shoulder usually over the right shoulder and tie it on the waist in the left side, although the diaconate stole is put the other way round."

"I got you." Said the priest.

"So to conclude the internal resistance to Botha's reforms, the ECC campaigned, inter alia, for an end to military conscription, withdrawal of troops from township, end to South Africa's participation in the war in Angola. Many white youths refused to join the army. The results for such actions were arrest and detention."

"So who were the members of the black sash." I asked.

"The members were white women who wore black sashes, black being symbolic for black people, they protested against apartheid. Black Sash was committed to giving humanitarian and practical support to victims of apartheid. So that's all about the internal resistance to Botha's reforms."

"Wow, I am impressed." George said.

"I think we should come again tomorrow, can we have an appointment with you Peter?" asked Luke.

"Yes of course, what time tomorrow?" he asked.

Luke looked at James, Bryan looked at Paul while Paul was looking at Peter, George was looking at me and I was looking at Peter the main man. It was at that time that I have notice the appearance of Paul and Peter; they looked alike in a way, as if they were some kind of twins, or relatives maybe.

"You decide Peter." Said James.

"How is 8am? Same place." He said.

"Now you're turning my house into a history lecture room." Commented Paul.

"That's not a problem, said Navirta from the Kitchen.

"Let's meet tomorrow then gentlemen." said Paul. The musician.

CHAPTER TEN

The International Response to Apartheid.

We then left Mr. Paul and Mr. Peter, and headed to our apartments. Sooner than expected, morning came, sunrise, cheering trees and hooters sounds in the District, slightly blowing breeze. As usual Sir James and Mr. Luke not forgetting Fr. Bryan came to pick us up.

"Chungu, have you noticed that we are now a team?" said George.

"What team are you talking about?" I asked.

"The five of us." He said.

"Wow, I did not notice that until now." I said.

"Good morning Chungu and George." Said Sir James.

"Good morning Mr. James, Mr. Luke and Fr. Bryan." We said.

"You're on time." Said Fr. Bryan.

"I am glad you are." responded James.

"Shall we hit the road? It's few minutes to 8 now." Said Luke.

We then arrived at Mr. Paul's house; Mr. Peter was already there, waiting to tell us more.

"Good morning gentlemen." Said Paul.

"Good morning to you all." Responded James.

"You're people of trust." Said Peter.

"Only if you knew." Silently said Luke.

"Shall we?" asked Paul.

"Yes, please." I said.

"Over to you Professor Peter." Said Paul.

"Now, yesterday we talked of the 'Internal Resistance' to Botha's reforms. Let's talk about the 'International Resistance or Response to apartheid general.'"

"Give us the information." George said.

"The international solidarity played a key role in dismantling apartheid. The UNO had declared apartheid as a crime against humanity. The Anti-Apartheid Movement was formed in Ireland by Kader Asmal, a South African exile living in Ireland."

"So far!" George said.

"He was exiled, that's the reason. The AAM spread…."

"That's Anti-Apartheid Movement George." I interrupted.

"Thank you Chungu." He said.

"You may continue Mr. Peter." Luke.

"The AAM spread to Britain and Scandinavian countries. It also started sports, cultural, economy and academic boycotts. So apartheid South Africa became a pariah state. Sports tours by South Africa teams were disrupted and could not take place. Western countries and companies withdrew their investments from South Africa- with devastating effects for economy. An intense campaign for the release of Mandela was started-the 'Release Madela Campaign.'"

"Wow." I sighed.

"So basically those were the International resistance to Botha's reforms of Apartheid."

"Interesting, indeed." I said.

"Why don't we talk about 'The Beginning of the End?'" said Peter.

"What was that?" asked George.

"In the 1980s South Africa experienced an economic recession. Economic sanctions and disinvestments crippled the economy further. Inflation skyrocketed, unemployment figures rose across all races. In 1985 a section of white businessmen met with the exile ANC leaders in Lusaka, Zambia. The ANC delegation was led by its president OR Tambo and the South African Business delegation was led by Gavin O'Relly, chairman of Anglo-American. There was a developing chasm/rift between the white politicians and major white businesses in the country. The National Party was virtually on its knees. Mass resistance intensified."

"The Beginning of the End. I like the sound of that." I said.

"What about the Crisis in the National Party Mr. Peter." George asked.

"Paul knows that one better than I do." Peter said.

"Oh yes! That's my league. Now, in 1989 August P.W. Botha suffered a minor stoke. He resigned as the leader of the National Party (NP) but remained the President of South Africa. Fredrik Willem de Klerk was elected leader of the NP- this created two centres of power within the ruling bloc. There was discontent in the NP about PW Botha's government- he had attempted to release Mandela with strict conditions in 1985, Botha rejected any form of contact with the ANC, South Africa was experiencing its worst economic recession, the country was ungovernable due to internal unrest- a state of insurrection had developed in the country."

"Did Botha resign on his own or there was influence somewhere somehow?" I asked.

"Well Chungu, there are rumors that he was in a way forced to do so. But he eventually did so. Amidst all of this PW Botha remained inflexible and autocratic. It is said that secretly Mandela and PW Botha met and Mandela advised him to release all political prisoners before any negotiations can start. Both refused! But in September 1989 Botha was forced to resigned and De Klerk became State President."

"Removed totally from power?" George said.

"Totally. Let's talk about the Civil Society Resistance in South Africa, 1970's-1980s."

"Steve Bantu Biko!" I said.

"The struggle for freedom was effectively crushed in the 1960's. The ANC, PAC, SACP and other organizations were banned. There was hopelessness and apathy amongst the oppressed masses. A period of a political lull engulfed South Africa. Black Consciousness ideas inspired a renewal of the struggle against apartheid."

"This is amazing!"George said.

"In 1968 Biko, Onkgopotse Abraham Tiro, Professor Barney Pityana, Ben Ngubane, Dr. Mamphela Ramphele broke away from the National Union of South African Students (NUSAS) and formed the South African Students Organization (SASO). They accused NUSAS of racial duplicity-acting as if they were against apartheid but continued to practice racial discrimination. SASO was exclusively for black students-whites were viewed as part of the problem."

"I was not aware of these things. It is indeed interesting." I said.

"I would like to know, what was the 'Black Consciousness'? asked Fr. Bryan.

"From the horse's mouth Bryan, 'Black Consciousness is an attitude of the mind and way of life, the most positive call to emanate from the black world for a long time.'"

"I think I am answered." Bryan said.

"BC aimed to…"

"BC for 'Black Consciousness' Eden. I said.

"I got it Chungu, will you stop assisting me now?"

"Alright, but don't forget. Okay?"

"I won't. Please carry on Paul."

"As I was saying, BC aimed to develop the self-worth of Black people. To imbue blacks with pride and self-reliance. Black consciousness can be defined as an attitude of the mind wherein Black people affirm themselves without depending on white people. The whites were regarded as part of the problem because they benefitted from the system of apartheid. BC sought to totally exclude whites from the struggle for the freedom of the Black people. So the BC was not advocating 'anti-whitism' so to speak, but sought to address the realities confronting blacks in South Africa. Also the BC gave hope to Black people, hope for humanity and hope for South Africa. This hope was expressed in slogans such as:

'Black is Beautiful'
'Black and Proud'
'Young, Gifted and Black'
'Black Man you are on your own.'"

"That's sounds like African Americans." George said.

"Do you now see the link between the two? You now see that the Black Americans were fighting for the very same thing with Black South Africans in their countries."

"My eyes are opened." I said.

"To answer your question again Bryan, BC aimed to free the mind of the black man so he can fight for what belongs to him. Black people should not feel inferior to whites. Solidarity with Coloureds and Indians was encouraged. Blacks had to be free from psychological oppression before being freed from physical oppression of living in a racist society. SASO was used as the vehicle to champion the BC philosophy."

"Any question?" Paul asked.

"I would like to the know more about the Role of Steve Bantu Biko, after leaving NUSAS and forming SASO, what happened thereafter?" George said.

"I like your question. I was about to talk about that. That means you're advance."

There was laughter in the room.

"Steve Biko left NUSAS and formed SASO, as I explained before. He was elected president of SASO in July 1969. He is regarded as one of the leading thinkers and activists against apartheid. He was only 30 years when he died. His writings are also published in the book 'I write what I like'. He started community self-help projects around King William's Town-like the Zanempilo Clinic at Zinyoka Village, Zingisa Education project. He also believed that racial integration can be possible if blacks and whites participated as equals in that process. Biko like Pityana challenged white supremacy and vowed to work for its downfall. Bantu became the preeminent pioneer of the BC philosophy; in 1973 he was banned and restricted to the magisterial district of King William's Town. Are we still together?"

"You tell the story Paul as it is." Said Peter.

"Blacks in South Africa and Blacks in America were all fighting: 'Non violence'; promoting 'black is beautiful... black pride... and so on and so forth. He believed that for blacks to attain liberation, they should not associate with whites. Black people must liberate themselves. He encouraged democratic participation in decision-making. During his presidency SASO grew rapidly and had a national footprint in all black universities. He was arrested, under the Terrorism Act, while travelling to Cape Town."

"That's very sad." I said.

"He was then taken to Port Elizabeth where he was detained and tortured. While critically injured from police torture, he was transported, naked, on the back of a police van to Pretoria. He then died in police custody."

"That's heart breaking." Said Eden.

"What happened after his death?" Asked James.

"Well, many people could not believe it. Professor Pityana, Dr. Ramphele and many more, were astonished. When the police minister James Thomas known as 'Jimmy Kruger', was asked about Biko's death he said, *'It leaves me cold.'*"

"He was indeed heartless!" James said.

"Thank goodness that not all the James' are like that."

Hahaha, we shared the laugh.

"Tell us about the BCM Paul." Luke said.

"Well, let me return the cables to Peter, I think he knows that better than I do."

"Come let us take a walk, down the street. I like to take a walk at this time of the day. Said Peter.

It was about the eleventh hour, close to mid-day. We then went outside, it was a beautiful day indeed, very silent, and calm.

"The BCM emerged from ethnic universalities in the late 1960's. It was not a single organization but an umbrella body of different organizations, instituted, churches, youth structures that believed and promoted black pride and self-reliance of black people. It was a philosophical front for organizations espousing BC ideology. An organization to be the central core of BCM was formed in 1971, and was called the Black Peoples Convention (BPC). BPC did not succeed in mobilizing support in Black communities. BCM was successful among high school students. Influenced by BC black workers organized into trade unions in defiance of anti-strike laws. Strikes became common-trade unionism was rejuvenated."

"From my own observation, the American 'Non- violence' was triggered by legends such as Albert Luthulu, Nelson Mandela, Steve Bantu Biko particular, Biko and the Black Consciousness Movement."

"Continue Sir. We're all ears." I said

"From the landing of Jan Van Riebeeck in 1652 at the Cape of Good Hope, in South Africa. Professor Mobogo Percy More, notes the Philosophical Basis of the Thought and Practice of Chief Albert Luthuli, Nelson Mandela and that of Steve Bantu Biko. So he says the 'Resistance to white colonization and domination has been violent. The Kaffir wars (which is regarded as derogatory to use, as equivalent to Niger or Negros in America) in the Cape, the Zulu wars, the Basotho wars, and the Bapedi wars are evidence of this violent struggle against colonization.'"

"Including the Xhosa wars." George added.

"Including the Xhosa wars, yes. Peter concluded.

"That may take us back to the Mfecane Wars." I said.

"Yes, indeed." Eden added.

"At times I forget that you're historians, I forgot that I am teaching experts here." Peter said.

"We all gave a laugh after that."

"Let me reference Prof. More again." Said Peter. "In 1906," he continued. "After the Bambata Rebellion, Africans came to accept the futility of violent struggle without weapons to match those of the oppressor."

"What was the Bambatha Rebellion Peter?" Asked Father Bryan.

"It was a Zulu revolt as they would explain it, against British rule and taxation in Natal, South Africa, that was in 1906. So the revolt was led by Bambatha kaMancinza, leader of the amaZondi clan of the Zulu people, who lived in the Mpanza Valley in KwaZulu-Natal, near the place known as Greytown."

"I see." Said Bryan.

"Gandhian non-violent resistance became a reasonable moral choice.

Chief Albert Luthuli (1898–1967), the bearer of the light (torch) as Prof. More would describe him, torch bearer of Gandhian non-violence, was first and foremost a believer in Christ Jesus and can be regarded as one of those rare men of nobility whose very existence proclaimed the dignity of human beings. He is described as a Christian liberal "realist" whose belief in the Gandhian philosophy of non-violent passive resistance was unquestionable. For Mabogo More, violence was not only destructive in essence but also inhumane, primitive, and uncivilized. So he was the ANC president at some time and Chief Luthuli was awarded the Nobel Peace Prize in around 1961. As a devout Christian, a Zulu chief, teacher, and politician, Luthuli did not only give himself completely to his people, he also had to face the ultimate issue of the choice between revolutionary violence and reconciliation, which no one who is both a Christian and leader of an oppressed people can escape."

"That's very unusual." I commented.

"In terms of Christian teachings, or Christianity as a whole, people can be reconciled with one another only insofar as they are reconciled with God. When reconciliation with God occurs, they give themselves in thought, word, and deed to the liberation of the oppressed and to the struggle against violence and dehumanization. Just as Jesus renounced violent methods as a means to liberation, Luthuli believed in "the spirit that revolts openly and boldly against injustice and expresses itself in a determined and non-violent manner."

"So he had challenges to be both a Christian and tribal leader?" James nodded.

"Of course, who said that if you're a Christian you'll never find difficulties, or if you are a tribal leader of clan leader for that matter will all go as you wish. Remember Jesus Christ did not promise smooth way of belief, but he told his disciples that, He sends them as lambs in the midst of wolves. Right Father? Peter confirmed.

"That's correct Mr. Peter." Said Fr Bryan.

"So Such a revolt, he held, remains the permanent duty of Christians. Again Professor Mobogo records in his work that Chief Albert Luthuli declared 'The Road to Freedom,' 'is via the cross' The cross symbolizes Christian heroism depicted by Christ's suffering and humiliation on the cross. Victory, on this view, is best brought about by suffering and adherence to the principles of non-violent resistance."

"He was very much attached to the faith huh!" said Fr Bryan.

"Very much so. The philosophy of non-violent resistance, borrowed largely from Gandhi, was therefore chosen precisely because it dealt with injustice in such a way as to reconcile the oppressed with the oppressor and to avoid sowing the seeds of hatred and bitterness. Non-violence, then, was a positive policy of reconciliation and love, a moral and ethical struggle for the good. Thus Luthuli declared: I have embraced the non-violent Passive Resistance technique in fighting for freedom because I am convinced it is the only non-revolutionary, legitimate and humane way that could be used by people denied, as we are, effective constitutional means to further our aspirations. Non-violence philosophy for Africa have been well articulated by Ali Mazrui and will not be dealt with in detail here."

"What, in more detail, is Mandela's position regarding the principle of non-violence?" I asked.

"Again, it is rightly fitting to refer to Prof. More. 'If Luthuli is described as a Christian pacifist, Mandela has been regarded as a humanist pacifist.' He says. Because of that, his pacifism has been nothing but a contributor to the famous Nobel Peace Prize, which was awarded to him. More again with other philosophers, put it clear in our minds that, pacifists, such as Gandhi and Martin Luther King Jr. Mandela personifies suffering under the most severe conditions and moral courage against an evil of a unique kind – apartheid. For this, he has earned widespread admiration. After spending 27 years in the notorious Robben Island prison. One effect of this sequence of events is that there is a tendency to perceive him only in terms of the post-Robben Island Mandela, a man of peace and reconciliation who preferred non-violence and negotiation as instruments of political liberation to revolutionary violence. The post-Robben Island Mandela, however, I would argue, is distinct from the pre-Robben Island Mandela. The latter was a radical.

"Peter why are you guys walking too fast? I am old now I can't walk fast as you. Please slow down." Complained Paul.

"We are not walking fast, not at all, we are just walking normal. Besides you are not older than me… just keep fit, walk with us."

"One year is the only difference in our age. I am old still."

Paul was really struggling behind us, we had to time and again walk and stop and wait for him.

"So there was also the government's response to BC. Initially the government welcomed the BC philosophy. They erroneously viewed it as encouraging separate development of races-therefore apartheid. BC leaders operated legally without state repression. As the BCM became stronger and Biko's speeches encouraged opposition to apartheid, the state became alarmed and targeted BCM leaders. Also the Apartheid state became BCM leaders from speaking in public. In 1974 eighty BPC members were detained under the Terrorism Act. In 1975 a year later, SASO was banned on university campuses. Biko was viewed as an enemy of the state. He was arrested and brutally murdered by the police in 1977, as explained earlier. The state was threatened by BCM."

"Mr. Peter are there any friends which you miss in South Africa? Maybe people who also influenced you to take an initiative to make a mark in the struggle. People you know personally perhaps." I asked.

"Come quickly Paul." Said Peter.

Leading the walk, it was myself, George and Peter, James and Luke where just behind us, behind them was Bryan and far back behind him it was the 'old man', Paul.

"Do you still remember Emmanuel Mabelane?" asked Peter.

"Yes, I still do." Responded Paul.

"Come let's sit under the tree." Peter said.

"Emmanuel was your best friend, very intelligent even at school. Well I don't know much about him. Why did you ask in the first place?"

"Emmanuel and I one time ago, went to the police station, from school. One of our short friends Mthokozisi Mthombeni had been arrested, accused of assaulting a police officer. So that day, Emmanuel came to me, Kagiso Semenya had joined us in the conversation, although he was scared to do what we were planning to do, but he managed to keep still. Emmanuel had suggested that we go and cause chaos in the police station so as to release our friend, I bet he missed him. But Emmanuel and myself went to the Police station leaving Kagiso to check the 'ghost' for us. When we arrived at the station, we told the police officers that the school was on fire, burnt by students, so we requested that they go and attend to that. Stupid enough, they all ran out to attend that fake case."

Hahaha

"You were naughty Peter." said James.

"So what happened thereafter?" George asked with enthusiasm.

"Well, seeing that they all went out, we then took all the cell keys and went to open all the cells. Although our intention was to release Mthokozisi, we ended up releasing everyone who was locked up. When we opened the cell in which Mthokozisi had been locked in, surprising enough, Mthokozisi had started to be the boss around there, people and prisoners were taking orders from him."

"But nevertheless, all happened as planned. Until we were all wanted by the police."

"I knew there was going to be something fishy after all." I said.

"The police were very angry and wanted to kill us, because when they arrived at the school there was no burning school, students were just going their way, and the school was over. Some students were even beaten up because just by seeing the police van you had to ran, and they too did so, but the police thought that they were the ones burning the school."

"Poor students." Luke commented.

"Mr. Peter what caused the Soweto Uprising?" I asked.

"Before I respond to that, let me tell you one more thing." Said Peter.

"One more thing!" nodded Paul.

"Now, it happened that, sometime ago, a young poor black street child who was muted, seated under a tree, saw a white woman passing by that tree. Now the woman was scared, because she only noticed the child while passing, which makes it clear that if she had noticed before she would have not passed by that tree. Now the young boy noticed something falling from the purse of the white woman, the boy then quickly picked whatever was falling from the purse, having the intentions to give the owner. The woman started to run like nobody's business. She ran as if it was her first time to do so. The boy did the same, chased the woman with a high speed, and now the woman started to cry out loud "HELP! HELP!" few moments after she cried, a group of both black and white men appeared from nowhere, seeing the boy chasing the woman, decided to attend the boy, beat him up until he was in the state of death. Just before he died, he took out the wallet which had fallen from the white woman's purse and just handed it over to them. Immediately after that, he passed on bleeding and smiling."

"Oh! No!"

"He was mute you said?" asked Fr Bryan.

"Yes Father. He could not speak, hence he chased the woman."

"That was the thing!" Shouted James. "Because he was black, they had to attack the poor boy, if he was white, the woman would have waited and see what the boy was up to. Maybe even give him money to keep his breath. That boy died because he was black, nothing more, nothing less."

"What happened to the woman then?" I asked.

"The men gave the woman the wallet which had fallen from her purse. She could not believe it. At first she tried to defend herself by saying the boy might have quickly stolen it when she was passing by. But her conscious spoke to her, and she started to cry. Anyway, let me answer your question again.

The BC had most support among high school and university students. To organize high school students the South African Students Movement (SASM) was formed. Black Students were subjected to Bantu Education system. The government spent 15 times more on a while learner that did on a black leaner. Black schools were under-resourced. Overcrowding in black schools-exacerbated by the scrapping of the standard six class at primary schools in 1975. Severe shortages of classrooms and teachers also had an impact. Curriculum was limited-blacks not prepared for certain professions. Under-qualified teachers-this led to poor results.

"So there were certain subjects or courses which blacks were allowed to study?" George asked.

"Yes, you can also say that. So students also rejected the political conditions in the township-lack of houses, unemployment, high inflation due to the hike in the price of oil in 1973 etc... students were also influenced by the successes of student uprising in countries like France and the CRM in USA."

"So that goes back to what I said to you few days ago, that students in countries influenced each other through new published and broadcast." Said Luke.

"The liberation of Mozambique and Angola also encouraged the students. SASM conducted political lectures for students."

"And the Introduction of Afrikaans language?" James said.

"Yes, thanks for raising that. Introduction of Afrikaans as a medium of instruction in black schools triggered mass demonstration and rejection of Bantu Education. Black students demonstrated against inferior education. So the even that was to follow changed the course of history in South Africa."

"That was no on at all." Said Luke.

"The imposition of Afrikaans triggered the students uprising, SASM held a meeting on 13 June 1976 and decided to hold mass demonstration on 16 June 1976. An action committee, Soweto Students Representative Council, was formed."

"Forming after forming." Said the priest.

"The committee was led by Tsietsi Mashinini. Slogans for the march were written on poster, for example "Down with Afrikaans!", "To hell with Bantu Education!" and so on.

"To hell with it, I also say so." Said Fr. Bryan.

"On morning of 16 June 1976 thousands of students marched to Orlando Stadium to hold a peaceful rally. They were dressed in their various uniforms."

"Approximately about how many students went?" asked James.

"About 5 000 students were marching down Vilikazi Street when police tried to stop them. In that rally it was loud and clear that, "WE DO NOT WANT AFRIKAANS" TO HELL WITH AFRIKAANS."

"AMEN." Sighed Luke.

"Also, it did not end there, the police ordered the students to disperse. But the students refused. So the police fired warning shots, teargas, and releasing police dogs. Then the police fired on the crowd with live ammunition. Hector Petersen was one of the first victims killed by the police."

"Oh, so that's the one who is well known now by being courageous enough." I said.

"That's the one. But not him alone, there are many unnamed courageous students. We know a little bit of them and some not at all, so angered by the actions of the apartheid government. A state of lawlessness engulfed Soweto. Soweto was burning. Many students were killed and others injured. News of the uprising spread to other townships and protest actions spread across the length and breadth of South Africa. The youth paved the way for a renewed fight against apartheid. The Apartheid State had a crisis on their hands."

"Speaking of the crisis, I remember something Peter", said Paul, "It was also a kind of crisis so to speak. When we were still students also, we were not courageous enough, like Petersen and others, so that was not the only march held in the country, there were also other marches small marches supporting that big and main march in Soweto. So the crisis which we faced, and few of my friends…"

"Emmanuel also." I interrupted.

"No Chungu, Emmanuel was not there that day. Or maybe, I can't remember well. But the two Gabriels, Gabriel Sefafe and Gabriel Lesetla were there with us."

"With us?" George said.

"Yes, myself, Mthokozisi, Vuyisa the son of the Abathembu, and Themba Khoza the 'wiseman' we called him. So the two angels looked the same like identical twins."

"The angels?" said Peter.

"The two Gabriels. I mean."

"Oh! I see the logic now. I think I know those guys" Said Peter.

"Sure you do, I remember introducing you to them. Well, back to the crisis, we had decided to have the two Gabriels as the 'van guard'."

"What's the van guard?" asked Fr. Bryan.

"Those who lead the march. So myself and the rest of the guys were the 'rear guards."

"Meaning you were behind the van guards?" asked Bryan.

"Yes, you follow the system Father. That's what I like about priests, they follow easily."

He then gave a small laugh; we managed to share it with him.

"So, as they were in front we noticed that it was not going to work."

"Why not?" I asked.

"Because they looked the same, and that if the police should see them as the van guards, they would be both arrested. But now we took one of them to be at the back, and indeed the police came, there was shooting and throwing of stones and objects. So after a day of two, the police were looking for Gabriel Lesetla, for he was the one in front, they did not know which Gabriel was it, so we said there are two Gabriels which one do you want? They could not distinguish the difference between the two, so they were so frustrated such that they wanted to arrest both of them." 'Over my dead body' Emmanuel or Themba said to the police. 'You are not being fair, why you want to arrest two people because they look alike.' He asked them.

"This Emmanuel was strong wasn't he?" I said.

"Maybe maybe not or maybe Themba was strong." Paul said.

"Maybe, maybe not." Said Peter.

CHAPTER ELEVEN

The coming of Democracy to South Africa

Still sitting under the tree, listening to the great historians, Peter and Paul.

"May I conclude this research by telling you about 'The Coming of Democracy to South Africa?" asked Peter.

"I would like to know how democracy came to South Africa."George Eden said.

"There are about ten main stages which led to the democracy. The first one was the beginning of the solution."

"That sounds philosophical." I said.

"Maybe it is philosophical. Nevertheless, let's begin with 'The Beginning of the Solution', the collapse of Union Soviet Socialist Republics and the ending of the Cold War brought about change in the world. The apartheid state lost support from Western countries-they saw no need to support Pretoria in the wake of the collapse of communism."

"Many things had happened during that time. I can tell." Said James.

"Of course, the world was not looking at Pretoria only; the collapse of the USSR was also in the brink. So USSR had been a prime backer of the ANC for quite some time. The ANC found itself in a weakened situation, without Russia's support. The Russians had withdrawn themselves. But the Russians that we eat at breakfast."

We all gave a laugh at that.

"Negotiations between the ANC and the NP Government became the only viable option to solve South Africa's political challenges."

"What the meaning of NP again?" asked George.

"You said I must not assist you in this, now you're asking again." I said.

"I was not asking you Chungu." He said.

"National Party." I answered.

"So the ANC set out pre-conditions before negotiations could take place, which was good in a way. So the pre-conditions were: The lifting of the State Emergency; the Unbanning of all banned political parties; Unconditional release of all political prisoners and of course the withdrawal of troops from the townships."

"So did that eventually happened?" I asked.

"Yes, the government did not really have a choice, because remember the was political unrest in the country, not only that but also the instability."

"It makes sense." I commented.

"The international balance of power left the ANC and the NP with no other option but to negotiate a political settlement."

"Do you still remember what NP stands for George?" I sarcastically asked.

"Yes, thank you Chungu." He said.

George was really bad when it comes to abbreviations, I don't know what had happened whether it was lost of memory. He used to have a good memory in Southern Africa, I believe in Russia as well. Maybe he was getting old.

"Secret talks were held with the exiled ANC by different interest groups from South Africa, for example Afrikaner business leaders, non-governmental organization and so on. The NP distanced itself from these meetings. PW Botha deployed his minister of justice, Kobie Coetzee to have exploratory talks with Mandela in 1985. These talks continued without the public knowledge. The NP leaders were not happy with PW Botha's reluctance to fully engage the ANC. So in 1989 FW de Klerk became president of the National Party and South Africa. De klerk met Nelson Mandela several times- culminating in the release of political prisoners like Walter Sisulu, Raymond Mhlaba, Ahmed Kathrada and others in October 1989."

"This is interesting. Now what I want to know is that, according to what you have just said, to me it seems like De Klerk was a kind of an opposite of Botha. I'm I correct." I said.

"I have to congratulate you Mr. African, you have it all. But now, many people even South Africans painted De Klerk with the same paint and brush. I can also tell, that De Klerk wanted some change in the country, some members of the ANC thought that he was also playing some schemes, but honestly he wanted to change South Africa, for whatever reason, he wanted the change.

"But listen until you hear more." Said Luke.

"You may continue Peter." Said Paul.

"Now let's look at the 'Unbanning of Political Organizations,' De Klerk committed his government to negotiations for a democratic South Africa. The political climate in South

Africa needed to be normalized. Such normalization could not take place if some organizations remained banned or illegal to be more precise."

"FW knew that very well." Said Paul.

"De Klerk and his cabinet held a special meeting in December 1989. On 2 February 1990, in his address to parliament, FW de Klerk announced the unbanning of the ANC, SACP, PAC and all subsidiary organizations. He also announced his commitment to release Nelson Mandela from prison."

"What did the parliamentarians say on that?" asked George.

"The Conservative Party of Andries Treurniht disapproved of the changes. They marched out of parliament."

"Wow!" said Fr. Bryan.

"The third stage was the 'Release of Nelson Mandela' uDalibhunga."

"I have been waiting for that one." Said George.

"The National Party government announced that Mandela would be released as promised. On Sunday, 11 February 1990, Nelson Mandela was released from Victor Verster Prison. With Mandela's release the country was gripped by a state of euphoria, triumph, hope, uncertainty and fear among certain sections of the white community. Impromptu, celebratory marches were witnessed all over the country and the world. The release of Mandela meant that South Africa would never be the same again and this even marks a turning point in the history of our country. The country was firmly on the road to democracy. The ANC held the biggest rally ever at the FNB Stadium to welcome home Mandela."

"And that was the release of Rholihlahla." Said Luke.

"What other stage Mr. Peter." Asked Fr. Bryan as he was changing sitting position, chasing the shade.

"'Talks about Talks.'" Peter said.

"Where those negotiations." I asked.

"Preface to negotiations rather. 'Talks about Talks' refers to the initial, exploratory, informal, preparatory discussions or talks between the African National Congress and the National Party government. The objective was to make preparations for 'real negotiations.'"

"Oh! I see now." I said.

"The first meeting took place in May 1991 in Cape Town. The two parties signed the historic Grootte Schuur Minute."

"What is that." Asked George.

"It was some kind of a vow or agreement to the 'Talks about Talks.'" Paul said.

"I get the idea now." I phrased.

"The second meeting took place in August 1991 in Pretoria. At this meeting the ANC announced that it would suspend its armed struggle indefinitely in order to give negotiations a chance."

"O dear!" exclaimed Bryan.

"So the parties signed the Pretoria Minute – which was a concrete commitment to negotiations for a democratic South Africa. The PAC accused the ANC for negotiating secretly with the government. The ANC counted that the PAC was free to engage the regime at will."

"The other stage was the 'Multi-Party Negotiations'."

"Where these the real negotiations?" asked George.

"Well this time around you can say that. But I would like to draw your attention to the 'Positions or standpoints of the National Party and the African National Congress regarding the content of negotiations."

"Hit it Mr. Peter!" I shouted.

"What was the National Party's standpoint?" Fr. Bryan asked with interest.

"The National Party and the National Party government wanted to engage in negotiations in order to reform the apartheid system on the basis of power sharing and to create a new order where the National Party still retained real political power. Also the National Party wanted protection of group rights and qualified franchise or voting, 'voting with certain conditions'. The main concern of the NP and the government was to protect while interests. I hope you are answered Bryan."

"I am Sir, and was the standpoint of the ANC?" Asked Fr again.

"The ANC wanted total destruction of the apartheid system. Total and complete transfer of power from the white minority to the progressive democratic majority. The ANC also demanded universal suffrage on the basis of one man, one vote on a common voters' roll. Above all, recongintion and protection of human rights through the adoption of a Bill of Rights."

"And what about the negotiations as the whole?" I asked.

"The NP and the ANC continued to work towards real negotiations. It was agreed that the process of negotiations should be as inclusive as possible. All parties should play a role."

"Did that happened?" George asked.

"There were leaders within the ANC who were skeptical and did not favour negotiations. Parties like the PAC,

AZAPO, and CP expressed their opposition to negotiations, for different reasons. On 20 December 1991 at the Johannesburg World Trade Centre, the first session of the multi-party negotiating convention was held. This convention was called the Convention for a Democratic South Africa, what became known 'CODESA'. A total of nineteen political parties attended."

"CODESA 1 you mean." Said Paul.

"Yes, CODESA 1 friend."

"How many CODESAS?" did they form?" I asked.

"Two. Judge Piet Schabort and Judge Ismail Mohamed jointly chaired CODESA 1. CODESA 1 agreed to have constitutional principles, that laid the foundation for a democratic constitution, drafted for adoption. Political parties also signed a Declaration of intent – pledging their commitment to productive negotiations. The plenary sessions of CODESA 1 established five working groups to deal with different matters. Real negotiations would take in the working groups. The Inkatha Freedom Party 'IFP' demanded that there be a delegation representing the Zulu king at CODESA."

"What a demand!" I exclaimed.

"This was highly contentious issue. At the conclusion of CODESA 1 Mandela reprimanded De Klerk in public after De Klerk accused the ANC of not being committed to peaceful negotiations."

"I wish I was there to hear that one." Commented Fr. Bryan.

"All parties agreed that an interim government be formed until a new constitution had been adopted. The fear was that the NP was playing a dual role of being both 'player and a referee.' However the interim government, known as the Transitional Council was not effective. So the NP government was still in effective control of state power. It was agreed that the multi-party negotiating plenary would meet in March 1992 as CODESA 2."

"Oh! I see now why there were two CODESA's, it didn't make sense at first." I said.

"Yes, so the seating of CODESA 2 was characterized by sharp differences between the ANC and the NP. These differences emanated from the various working groups. Not much was achieved during CODESA 2. Violence began to pose a serious threat to negotiations. Another stage was the 'The Threat of Violence to Negotiations.'"

"Threat of violence to negotiations!" said George.

"The negotiation process was threatened by the growing political violence in the country. The outbreak of violence was precipitated by political differences between the ANC the IFP. In addition, right-wing groups, such as the Conservative Party, AWB and some homeland leaders, protested against the negotiation process. The government did not deal decisively with the problem of violence. Negotiations were under severe stress. De Klerk's government was under pressure locally and internationally."

"I can imagine that pressure!" said James.

"The NP government announced that a referendum will be held to test the views of the white electorate and to get a mandate as to whether negotiations should continue."

"Tell me now Peter, where these negotiations the ones that had accused Madiba as to be a sellout of South Africa?"

"Yes, that's correct. Very much so. But I describe that as lack of knowledge hence now I am glad that there are people like you to seek for the true history of our lands and times.

People need to tell the history as it is, then people will judge it by themselves and for themselves. Try not to be bias when telling history, painful as it maybe, but tell it all."

"He sounds like the Great Kamala." George whispered to my ears.

"Indeed you are right." I responded softly.

"The referendum was held in March 1992, and the results were 68,6% in favour of negotiations."

"Wow, I did not expect that." Luke said.

"I understand why Luke. So the NP government felt that the referendum results gave them a clear mandate to continue negotiations. Natal became the site of extreme violence between the IFP and the ANC. The violence in Natal became a battle for territorial supremacy between the IFP and the ANC. The ANC established 'Self Defense Units (SDU's) and the IFP established 'Self Protection Units' to protect themselves and their communities. Violence spread to the PWV area now known as Gauteng province. Hostels, where migrant workers stayed, became IFP strongholds and where in conflict with nearby townships."

"If I am following, the hostels where 'mainly' for the IFP and the townships 'mainly' for the ANC. is that what you are saying Mr. Peter? I asked.

"Yes, Chungu." He said. "The hostels mainly stayed the Zulus, and in the townships lived the Xhosas mainly."

"It make sense." George said.

"Hostels for IFP and townships for ANC were locked in perpetual conflict. The NP government seemed to lack the will to end violence. It referred to it as "Black-on-black" violence."

"So the conflict continued between the IFP and the ANC?" asked Fr. Bryan as if he was waking up.

"Yes, it continued and the government wanted nothing to do with it. The NP did not want to get involved, for they referred to it as black-on-black violence. So the ANC and the many in the country accused the government of complicity in violence."

"What was the meaning of that again Peter?" asked Paul.

"The government maintained its innocence, but did very little to stop violence. When it acted it showed biasness towards the IFP."

"Oh yes! I remember that. The NP favored the IFP and had assisted them in the conflict, but hiding themselves at the same time. Just like the police brutality in the States. The longer the violence continued the more the credibility of negotiations gets eroded and this was beneficial for the NP government." Paul added.

"This was tougher than I thought." Said George."

"There were some incidents of political violence." Continued Peter. "For example, in 1990 violence flared up in the Thokoza Township between ANC and IFP supporters. The response of the police was that they would not get involved in a political conflict between the Xhosas and the Zulus. The Sebokeng massacre, 3 September 1990 – riot police killed eleven people, 23 more died in conflict between the IFP and ANC. On 12 May 1991, 27 people killed in Swanieville informal settlement by IFP hostel of 17 June 1992 armed IFP members 300 from the KwaMadala hostel attacked the township of Boipatong in Johannesburg. A total of 46 people were attacked and murdered and many injured. This became known as the Boipatong massacre."

"There is no difference between our history and the that of South Africans." Said Fr. Bryan.

"Many say so Father, and now I tend to agree with that." Said George.

"Some other incidents of the massacre alleged that they saw white men among the IFP attackers." Said Peter.

"Is that what you were referring to Mr. Paul?" I asked.

"Yes, that's what I was referring to Chungu." He responded.

"Yes, Paul is right, that's what he was explaining to you earlier. Mandela accused De Klerk of doing nothing to stop violence."

"Again?" I said.

"No, remember, Mandela first reprimanded FW de Klerk, he did not accused him, but this time, he was not only reprimanding him, but accused him of not doing anything to stop the conflict. De Klerk was still the president of the country, so he had a mandate to stop the violence. At least do something."

"Maybe he was bit nervous about it, or maybe it was best for him not to do anything about it. Or maybe he was really supposed to do something, since there was a gorilla hand involved, and that is to say since there was 'something fishy.'" Said Fr. Bryan.

"Further eye-witness accounts claimed that the police had escorted the IFP attackers."

"Is that so!" Exclaimed George.

"Mandela and the ANC were convinced that a 'Third Force' was involved in the violence, what Bryan was referring to as the gorilla hand. So the intention of the so called 'Third Force' was to destabilize the country and to ensure that CODESA failed. On 7 September 1992, the soldiers of the Ciskei homeland, under Brigadier Oupa Gqozo, shot and killed 29 people during an ANC march to Bhisho what is now known as the Bhisho massacre. This was following after the massacre in Boipatong."

"Massacre after the other." Said Luke.

"Given the level of violence in the country and the failure of the government to act, the ANC announced that it was suspending all talks with the NP and NP government. Negotiations were on hold! Now the ANC accused the NP government of complicity in the two massacres, not doing anything about it. The CODESA talks on the other hand were put on hold indefinitely! The ANC then announced that a program of 'Rolling Mass Action'. Marches were held in various towns and cities. The ANC again accused the government of negotiating in bad faith. The uKhongolose as sometimes called, meaning 'The Congress' also used this opportunity to flex its muscle and to touch base with its constituency, and the country was on the brink of civil war."

"What's another stage again?" asked Peter.

"The 'Resumption of Negotiations'." Said Paul.

"Please continue Paul." Said Peter.

"Even though formal negotiations had been suspended, the ANC and the NP continued to engage privately. Both the ANC and the NP remained committed to negotiations. A channel for behind the scene talks was opened. The key negotiations were Roelf Meyer of the NP and Cyril Ramaphosa of the ANC. Again, the two parties agreed, in spite of their political difference, that the negotiations process was the only viable option."

"I am hungry!" said Peter.

"Oh my goodness, its lunch time already. My apologies gentlemen." Paul said.

"Shall we?" asked Peter.

"Yes, please."

Surprisingly, James was sleeping like nobody's business.

"James!" called Luke.

"So we fought in the apartheid!" James said without making any sense."

"Mr. Peter, please tell us your experience in the struggle." I said.

"Well what can I say, I am not a hero."

"Don't say that Peter." Said Luke.

Again, the procession to Paul's house did not change, in front it was myself George and Peter, behind us was Fr. Bryan James and Luke, far behind them was the 'old' man Paul.

"Well, let me just share what we did." Peter said. "Hmmhrr!" He cleared his throat. "It was December if I am not mistaken, one of Paul's friends named Obakeng Masethla, joined our crew."

"It seems like you and Paul were not friends in those days. Or maybe you were not so close." George said.

"Not that we were not friends, it's just that each had his crew, and that we had to control those crew. We were organizing and leading marchers in towns and townships, but at times were would emerge and make one thing. Some other times we would fight for we would disagree to some of the things."

"Such as?" I asked.

"Such as leading the march, who should be that van guard who should be what and so on and on... "

"But I believe in most of the times you would agree and work together." George said.

"That's correct Eden. Now back to the story. Obakeng had flew from Paul's 'army' and had joined mine, which also led to the tension between Paul and myself. But nevertheless, one day we went to steal one of the yellow police vans, we wanted actually to burn it. One thing that triggered that was the arrest of Obakeng's brother and Akhona's siblings. We arrived at the station, and we saw the vans in the parking lot. One of the police officers came out, immediately he got angry, why! Because we were black, that was always the case. So he had asked us what were we doing in at the station, we told him that we wanted to see how the police operates at the station, and how do they arrest people. Surprisingly enough, Kagiso Semenya and Akhona Ndyawe were already in the police vehicle, how! Nobody remembers. Then the next thing was them starting the engine, as the officer was trying to get us out of the station, the van reversed to us."

"Who was driving the van Mr. Peter?" I asked.

"I can't remember Chungu, but what I remember is that as the van was coming towards us near the gate, the police thought that it was one of the officers, as he was giving way for the van, one of them, whoever was seating on the passenger seat, opened the door and had the officer dragged down, immediately we all got in and left with the police van."

"What were your plans for the van." I asked.

"It was a police van for goodness sake, it's easy to identify." George added.

"Our plans were to make fool of the police officers, we were angry for their actions. But mainly we wanted to burn the vehicle."

"Did you do it!" asked George.

121

"Yes, we did it. We drove until we were far away from the townships. We then burnt it there. Akhona was the one who burnt it, I could see he wanted to do it himself, Obakeng also stood in front of it with tears running down his cheeks. If you could read their eyes, one would simply say, they were saying, 'burn you demon.' But what! Burning that vehicle was like burning the Devil, the prince of fire, it did not do any harm to those guys, instead it gave them a fire signal to easily follow the fire, and they saw their van burning there."

"Where are you during that time." I asked.

"What time?"

"The time of their arrival." George added.

"We were in the bush. We ran as if we were in the race. Until we were tired. We did not go to school, because we were 'wanted'. But we wanted to show them actually the Brightness of Darkness of an African. We wanted to show them that we are also people, and that there was no difference between us, it was only the colour of the skin, and the quality of our hairs, having that silky hair did not make them superior or clear than the rest of us!"

On that note, we arrived at Paul's house, having him limping behind. Again the music was so loud, the first daughter of Paul, was blowing the lute, the wife was dancing with the youngest son, and the other son was, busy dancing while arranging the dinner table, and the youngest daughter was playing the guitar. When I looked back, Paul was also dancing, singing one of their composed songs, which titled 'The Lover of my Heart', surprisingly Peter had known the lyrics, for he was their producer. He did not waste time; he went to play the piano and echoed them. Now the history of their music began in the time of the struggle, where they wrote together (Peter and Paul) the songs against the struggle. It was their life, it was their passion.

"Lunch will be served in no time." One of the sons said.

"Thank you son." Paul said while seating down. "Gentlemen you may have a seat, this is your home also."

After few moments, we had lunch together, the whole family. Which reminded me that last big lunch in Africa, in the palace of Chief Lesetla Mokoena II. Just next to the castle room. It was bringing those unforgettable memories. After that big lunch, we resumed with our topic.

"To wrap up everything we discussed earlier, what were we talking about?" asked Paul.

"I can't remember." Said Peter.

"I think we were talking about the resumption of negotiations and Roelf Meyer being the key negotiator of the NP and Cyril Ramphosa of the ANC." I said.

"Thank you Chungu." Peter said. "You have a good memory." He added. "At the end of September 1992, Mandela and De Klerk met and singed the 'Record of Understanding.' The Record of understanding was an undertaking to remove all obstacles in the way of formal negotiations. Both parties agreed that there was a need for democratic constitution making body. The eighth stage of the coming of democracy to South Africa was the 'Sunset Clause' and Compromise. The Record of Understanding led to better working relations between the ANC and the National Party. The ANC and NP assumed responsibility and leadership for the process of negotiation. The multi-party negotiations were resumed in a re-structured form. Joe Slovo (SACP and ANC member) argued that the ANC needed to make certain compromises to ensure the success of negotiations. He argued that the ANC was not dealing with a defeated NP, therefore a complete seizure of power would not be possible."

"That is true. Totally true." Said Luke.

"So Joe Slovo proposed that there should be a 'sunset clause' in the constitution. This will be affected in a period of transition from the apartheid system to a truly democratic system. This would be based on some form of power sharing. The 'sunset clause' would protect Afrikaner bureaucrat's jobs, senior army and police personnel to serve under the new government, NP politicians to serve in the democratic government. Slovo stated: 'We can win political office, but we won't have political power.'"

"Mr. Peter what would power sharing mean?" George asked.

"Power sharing would be on the basis of proportional representation in the government, or cabinet if you like. Like what he said about the complete seizure of power from the white minority to the black majority, was not possible, he was suggesting that these two parties work together in office. Power sharing would be based on the number of votes, parties received at the general elections."

"What we see in the parliament today." James said.

"It was further agreed that all parties who achieved a minimum of 5% in the general elections will be entitled to representation in government. The country would have two deputy presidents, black and white.

"You sound like Michael Jackson, 'Black-White'." George said.

"Although it was 'Black or White.'" Paul said.

"Oh! Yes, you are right, 'Black or White.'" I said.

"These proposals were broadly accepted and formed the basis of the new process of negotiations. Now the sunset clause became the foundation of the new process of multi-party negotiations. It was agreed that the first democratically elected government will be called a **G**overnment of **N**ational **U**nity GNU. In early 1993 formal multi-party negotiations resumed. This time the process was called the Multi-Party Negotiating Process. Technical Committees were consisting of expects to attend to matters of detail. Not everybody was happy process as it unfolded. Some parties and organizations felt left out. Certain events again threatened the march to democracy. The new Multi-Party Negotiating Forum adopted a mechanism to break any deadlocks in the process of negotiations. This was called- sufficient consensus- which meant that if the ANC and NP agreed on any issue it would be taken there was enough agreement to proceed."

"It didn't matter about other parties." I asked.

"Well not that it did not matter, it's just that, the two main bulls was the ANC and the NP. The ninth stage of the Coming to Democracy to South Africa was the 'Multi-Party Negotiations under threat."

"Not again!" Said George.

"Yes, so the following events posed a threat to the resumed multi-party negotiations: The Assassination of Chris Hani."

"Oh, yes, I forgot about him already." I said.

"That was 10 April 1993 when he was murdered, Chris Hani was the secretary general of the SACP, and prominent leader of the ANC and chief of staff of uMkhonto wesizwe. The killer was Januz Walusz – a member of the AWB. The country was on the brink of anarchy and civil war. De Klerk was unable to offer leadership. Mandela was requested to address the nation on national television. He appealed for calm and reason. He said the only way the government could save the country from the brink of war was by announcing the date for democratic elections."

"True!" James exclaimed.

"This event ushered in a state of dual power in South Africa – with De Klerk as the *de jure* heard of state and Mandela as the *de facto* leader of the country."

"What was that thought?" Luke asked.

"It meant that, FW de Klerk was the leader by name and position, but Mandela was the one who could stabilize the situation in the country."

"It makes sense." Luke concluded.

"The NP government announced that the date for elections as 27 April 1994. Another threat was the 'AWB invasion of World Trade Centre'. In June 1993 the AWB invaded the World Trade Centre while negotiations were in session."

"What!" Exclaimed the priest.

"They used an armored vehicle to crash through a glass partition into the building."

"They meant business, huh!" I shouted.

"They were something else." Said George.

"Inside the AWB created chaos and even assaulting some of the delegates. No AWB member was ever arrested for this incident. Until present day."

"Why? Is it because they were white." I asked.

"Most probably. The government turned a blind eye to the situation."

"Another incident was the IFP march to Shell House. On 28 March 1994 the IFP marched to the headquarters of the ANC, Shell House also known as Luthuli House. The IFP wanted to show its opposition to the path of negotiations.

Chaos resulted – ANC security shot and killed 19 IFP supporters. This further strained the relations between the ANC and the IFP. The IFP also declared that it will not take part in the elections."

"Oh! This IFP…" I said.

"The last stage which is the tenth one, was 'The Elections and the Government of National Unity. 27 April 1994, the day that many South Africans will never forget. The country went to elections – the first democratic elections ever in South Africa. The IFP eventually agreed to participate in the elections. The ANC won the elections with a 63% majority. Nelson Mandela became the first democratically elected president of South Africa. The Government of National Unity governed the country. The GNU would be in place for the first years. In 1996 a new constitution was adopted and it contains a chapter on fundamental human rights. The government adopted the **R**econstruction and **D**evelopment **P**rogram, what became known as the RDP, to address social and economic injustices created by apartheid."

"Alright gentlemen, I think we should call it a day." Said Luke.

"But I have not yet told you about the TRC." Said Peter.

"Yep! We'll come tomorrow morning to wrap up everything."

"Don't worry Peter, they'll come tomorrow." Said Paul.

We then travelled back to the city. To where we resided. The research we were doing was in a way an eye opener, it was giving facts and roots of racism and discrimination which happens around the world. Nothing more happened that day, I appreciate a friend like George, who wants nothing but to see the world as a better place for all.

"Chungu." George called.

"Yes George."

"How would you describe prejudice?" he asked.

"Well, Naomi Boakye, Riette Pretorius and Tobie van Dyk in their book 'Academic reading', explain it as to be a negative evaluation of an entire group of people, that is typically based on unfavorable 'often wrong' ideas about the group. I don't know if that answers your question or not."

"Personally?"

"I would say, negative racial attitudes and judgments, not all, but most." I answered.

"Then what causes it." He further asked.

"Again, they refer to the causes as being different 'theories.' So many things or theories have varied that prejudice can be viewed in many Connors. For example, it can be examined within an individual, between individuals within a group. Well we can talk about many things, like 'reasonable racism' or even 'macro-aggressions'"

"And the theories?"

"They talk about 'Social learning theory' which they explain as the society having an impact for one to learn all these negative acts. Children for example, they learn these from their parents, no child is born racists, or xenophobic or whatever."

"Another?"

"Another would be the 'Motivational theory' a theory they explain as to be motivated, to succeed also to get ahead and to provide for basic as well as high-level emotional need. Another one is the 'Cognitive theory', in this theory, they say people think about individual and group they come from as a way of organizing the world. And the last theory would be a 'Personal theory', and that is to say some people develop prejudices because they have a prejudice-prone personality."

We the on the following day went back to Mr. Paul's house, who was indeed good in putting the struggles into understanding.

"Good morning gentlemen, please take a seat." said Paul.

The whole research crew was the, including the priest, Fr. Bryan. Peter was already there waiting for us, his big lens glasses.

"What topic are we covering today?" asked the old man.

"We were to talk about the TRC." I said.

"Oh yes! Tell me when you are ready."

"We were born ready Mr. Peter. Just lead the way and we shall follow." George said.

"Now, let's talk about the 'Truth and Reconciliation Commission'. So this was the only medicine to heal the wounds of the struggle, the wounds of apartheid. We need also to look at the questions which mainly came up during and after the TRC hearings. Again, we must understand that, at least in South Africa there was this TRC, to heal whatever wounds which needed to be healed."

"What are some of those questions Mr. Peter." Asked Bryan.

"There are a number of them. One of the main questions was that: 'Why was it necessary to have the TRC?'"

"And the answer to that?" I asked.

"The government of National Unity made provision for the appointment of the TRC. The main purpose was to heal the country from conflict of the past. To ensure that the country did not descend to a civil war and anarchy. Mandela saw it as a tool to drive reconciliation. The TRC was led by Archbishop Desmond Tutu (Chairman) and Dr Alex Borine (Vice Chairman). It had other commissioners and advisors."

"So it was also a 'Black and White' thing. Having Tutu and Borine as heads of the TRC, like Mandela made Thabo Mbeki his first vice president, and De Klerk as his second."

"That was also the process of healing, on it's on. Like in the Bible, the Jews did not expect Jesus to be the Messiah, simply because in their minds, they were expecting a 'King' with military army and all those sorts of political powers. Not someone who was born in their watch, by a carpenter, although they have seen his miracles being performed in their presence. You would agree with me Father Bryan, you know the stuff better than I do."

"That's correct Peter." He responded.

"They did not believe even those who were healed by him. So the same thing happened to Mandela, that people had hoped that Mandela will once in office announce the day for revenge, where black majority would go and attach the white minority. Another question was that: 'What were the main objectives of the TRC?'"

"We are listening Mr. Peter." I said.

Again, Sir James was sleeping in one of the double couches in the family room.

"James!" Shouted Luke.

"Leave him Luke, he must be tired." Said Paul.

"At this time of the day? Tired!" complained Luke.

"Probably he did not sleep last night, for whatever reason. Please leave him alone."

"You may continue Mr. Peter." Said the priest.

Fr Bryan was listening attentively as if he was indeed in a lecture room. He really enjoyed the combination of the American and South African history, the link between the two and why we can literary say 'one country is better than the other in this manner.

"To examine human rights abuses committed by those who supported apartheid and by those who opposed it. To promote national reconciliation and reconciliation between perpetrators and victims. To offenders/ perpetrators the opportunity to fully disclose their acts and to offer victims the opportunity to forgive the perpetrators. To offer amnesty and immunity from prosecution to all those who made full disclosure of their actions before the commission. To offer, where necessary and appropriate, monetary compensation to victims or their families. To promote nation building. To build a nation that is not founded on hatred and the desire for revenge. Also another question was: 'What preferred option in dealing with the past?' In dealing with the country's painful past the democratic government wanted a lasting and a healing process. The experience of the Nuremberg Trials after WWII was discounted by South Africa. It could lead to a divided country. The government looked at the various truth commissions that had been established in Latin America. The TRC was based on the model of a similar commission in Chile. The GNU wanted a process that will promote reconciliation and nation building. Retributive justice was not preferred as this could lead to more polarization. Instead the government favoured restorative justice. The TRC was not a court of law but an attempt at reconciliation."

"Did the TRC have any structure or something?" Asked George.

"The TRC had three committees: *'Committee on Human Rights Violations'*, which was to hear people's stories, to hear victims relate their experience of their rights being violated, to investigate each case fully, over 21 000 victims gave statements before this committee. And another was *'Committee on Amnesty'* which could grant amnesty to perpetrators of gross human rights abuses. Perpetrators appeared before this committee. Amnesty would be granted if the committee was satisfied that there was full disclosure and that the actions were politically motivated. The third one was *'Committee on Reparations and Rehabilitation* which investigated the testimonies of victims. Gave support and awarded reparations to victims. Compensation/ reparations for suffering and loss."

"And how did the TRC go, all together?" asked Fr Bryan.

"The TRC hearings were held in all provinces of South Africa. The first hearing was held in East London, in the Eastern Cape. TRC heard terrifying stories from victims and perpetrators alike. Some were well-known instances of killing of political activists, e.g. assassination of Griffiths and Victoria Mxenge, the death in police custody of Steve Biko, assassination of Chris Hani and many others. The Mxenge family opposed Captain Dirk Coetzee's application for amnesty for the killing of Griffiths Mxenge. The Biko and Mxenge families opposed the granting of amnesty and refused to forgive the perpetrators. Some high profile leaders refused to appear before the TRC, e.g. PW Botha. Some perpetrators showed utmost remorse for the crimes they committed. Former Minister of Law and Order, Adriaan Vlok washed the feet of Rev. Frank Chikane as a sign of his desire for forgiveness. Of course you would understand that Fr, the true meaning of washing the feet of another person, as you do it also on Holy Thursday, on the day of the last supper of the Lord Jesus, when he himself washed the feet of his own disciples, and he later took bread and broke it, gave thanks to the Father in heaven and gave the bread to his disciple, he said all that should be done in his memory, those who believe in him. So Adriaan Vlok knew exactly what he was doing. He knew that Chikane would not refuse as long as he called himself the servant of God. The Amnesty Committee had the right to subpoena witnesses to appear before it."

"Was the TRC a success or not?" I asked.

"The TRC had both positive and negative aspects. The Positive Aspects of the TRC was that the Truth and Reconciliation Commission served the purpose of confronting the evils of apartheid. It allowed the transition to democracy to be peaceful and non-violent. Public hearing helped to heal the country. Hearings were covered in both print and electronic media even whites could not claim ignorance about human rights abuses. It served a cathartic purpose gave emotional relief to those who testified in public. A process of healing and forgiveness between victim and perpetrator began. Families were able to know about their loved ones, what happened to them, where their remains were buried etc. this resulted in families having closure. Afrikaners could come to terms with the horrendous acts their government had committed on their behalf. The TRC made a tremendous effort to place the truth on record. It may not have been the whole truth. The TRC was able to reveal to a great extent the evils committed by the apartheid government torture of prisoners, state's sponsored death squads, lies, cover-ups, corruption, injustice etc. TRC also exposed human rights violation within the ranks of the liberation movements, ANC and PAC. Foundations for national healing and nation building were firmly in place."

"You said there were also negative aspects, what were they." George asked.

"The Negative Aspects of the TRC was that not everybody was happy with the TRC. Some people believed that there should have been war crimes tribunals to prosecute the offenders. Many white people believed that the TRC was a witch-hunt to punish whites. Others especially the victims or their families believed that the TRC was re-opening wounds that were beginning to heal. Victims or their families wanted justice rather than the truth. Perpetrators must pay. Not all victims were willing to forgive. Many people felt the TRC ignored the damage done to generations of South Africans. Amnesty provisions of the TRC were heavily criticized. It was infuriating to see the perpetrators walking free simple because they made a public confession. Many victims held the view that many perpetrators appeared before the TRC in order to escape arrest. Reparations were the greatest weakness of the TRC. Many victims had not received due compensation. The government maintained that all black people suffered under apartheid compensating a few would be immoral. High profile leaders refused to come and give testimony before the TRC, PW Botha, top ANC leaders, high command structures of MK, Mangosuthu Buthelezi."

"MK?" Asked George.

"UMkhonto weSizwe George." I said.

"So Botha never appeared before the hearings." Bryan asked.

"Yes, and that is why people ended up asking those kind of questions and saying lot of other things. People of the Republic of South Africa 'RSA', felt that the TRC was only wounding the healing wounds, because people were begging to forget what had happened, but now the TRC was again reversing the thing. Many also felt that, it was not inclusive at all, and had left the hearings. De Klerk's testimony before the TRC was viewed as less than honest. The lack of proper reparations and failure of the TRC to force high profile leaders to give testimony seriously challenged the model of restorative justice. Atrocities involving the IFP were largely ignored. TRC paid little attention to economic effects of apartheid. Led to divergent views in the country."

After spending hours at Mr. Paul's house, we had come to a conclusion that there was nothing different at all in the RSA and USA history, in terms of segregation, racism, inequality and even police brutality. They should have used hospitality over brutality, they should have used love over hatred, although hatred is not the opposite of love, but indifference is. They should have used accompaniment over accomplishment, they should have used hearts over stone hearts. They should have prayed to have eyes that see good in black people, ears that hear a human voice, mouths to speak good of them; hearts that understood the situation and above all, they should have prayed to have eyes that see humans than animals.

The way people treat each other around the world, is not at all pleasant. It is inappropriate; it is a grave misunderstanding. We are more than what we think we are, but how can we see light if we have our eyes closed? We too Africans we have it all, we have the brains that they have, the same muscles that they have, the same strength that they have and the same vision that they have. A white friend of mine sometime ago had reprimanded in public a black friend of ours for pronouncing an English word incorrectly. I was personally devastated by that. I asked the white friend, 'how many languages can you speak?' "One." He responded. I then asked the black friend the same question. "Six" he said. Hence we say today 'The Brightness of Darkness of an African. Not speaking good English or any colonial language does not mean we are inferior to other races; we black people who obtain PhD's in their own languages. There are more educated, intelligent black people than white people. We are one; it's only the matter of the skin. Nothing more nothing less. We have to work together and say like Runaine James Radine of the Diocese of Port Elizabeth #RacismMuustFall. Not in the future, but now! All races are racist, but some races are more racists than others.

I urge all Africans to learn how to love, I urge all people to learn how to love. We are one therefore we share the same humanity, we might come from different continents, but still we are humans. There is no race which is superior to the other, or inferior to the other. We need to treat one another as such. We would all change the world only if we were willing; by teaching what we were taught.

I might have been born at night, but not last night. I have a purpose, you have a purpose we have a purpose therefore let us not take things for granted. Everything we do count. "Do unto someone as you would like to be done unto you." I believe that it is better to be loved deeply than wildly, if we love wildly our love would quickly reach the end, but if we love deeply, we would be building a proper foundation of love. We cannot change the past, but we can fix the present and we can change the future. "May GOD bless AFRICA." May God bless the world?

Work References in this book

Desai, A. G. 1996. *Arise ye Coolies: Apartheid and the Indian, 1960-1995*. Johannesburg: Impact Africa Publishing.

Heunis, J. 2007. *The Inner Circle*. Johannesburg: Jonathan Ball Publishers.

https://www.history.com/topics/black-history/central-high-school-integration [cited 9 August 2018]

https://www.sahisto ry.org.za/article/1983-constitution-and-new-dispensation [cited 11 August 2018]

https://www.sahistory.org.za/article/1956-women%E2%80%99s-march-idara-akpan [cited 9 AUGUST 2018

Nenzani, C. H. 2015. The Coming of Democracy. Bhisho: Bhisho High School. [Unpublished lecture notes].

Nenzani, C. H. 2015. The Release of Nelson Mandela. Bhisho: Bhisho High School. [Unpublished lecture notes].

Omond, R. South Africa's Post-Apartheid Constitution, 1987, Third World Quarterly, Vol. 9, No. 2, After Apartheid (Apr., 1987), pp. 622-637

Spence, J.E, *South Africa: Reform versus Reaction*, 1981, The World Today, Vol. 37, No. 12 (Dec., 1981), pp. 461-468

James Yamkela Qeqe

Welsh, D. 2009. *The Rise and Fall of Apartheid.* Johannesburg: Jonathan Ball Publishers.

Welsh, D. Constitutional Changes in South Africa, 1984, Vol. 83, No. 331 (Apr., 1984), pp. 147-162

Wiredu, K. 2004. *A companion to African philosophy*: Malden. Blackwell Publishing Ltd.

https://thetwopathways.blogspot.com/2018/03/blinded-by-evolution.html

http://www.minerva.mic.ul.ie/vol10/Hegel.pdf